L. D. Palmer

Aid and Guide to Family Worship

L. D. Palmer

Aid and Guide to Family Worship

ISBN/EAN: 9783337291389

Printed in Europe, USA, Canada, Australia, Japan

Cover: Foto ©Lupo / pixelio.de

More available books at **www.hansebooks.com**

CONSISTING OF

Scripture Lessons, Songs, and Prayers.

COLLECTED AND ARRANGED BY
L. D. PALMER.

NASHVILLE, TENN.:
SOUTHERN METHODIST PUBLISHING HOUSE.
1886.

THE PURPOSE OF THIS BOOK.

No religious duty is more emphatically urged by evangelical Churches upon their members, and perhaps no one is more generally neglected, than family worship. Religious parents recognize it as a duty, and many of them have an inclination to discharge it. Some commence it, and in a short time leave it off in violation of their convictions.

It is well to consider what leads to such a common neglect of a duty recommended by the Church and admitted by the member. The case is generally about as follows: At a regular or revival service the preacher presents the duty of family worship, and impresses the average layman that he should read the Scriptures and pray with his family night and morning. With the encouragement of his wife, he determines to begin it. After the day's work is over, she gets the family together and hands him the Bible. With so much material before him, he scarcely knows how to select a suitable lesson. He finds many of the chapters too long, and is at a loss where to begin or where to stop so that his family may be impressed and benefited by the lesson. Perhaps the time is short, and not being as familiar as he ought to be with the Scriptures, he stumbles upon some part not appropriate to such an occasion, and finds himself embarrassed. He feels the need of a list of selections made by older Christians, which they have found well suited to such a service. Perhaps he or his family are inclined to sing, but the hymn-book may be out of place, and if in place he does not know what to select from such a mass, and so this beautiful part of the worship is usually omitted. He is not accustomed to extemporaneous speech, but with a heart full of gratitude he kneels with his family, and thanks God for the blessings of daily life, and asks for their continuance; remembers the absent loved ones; prays for his Church and for all classes of men. In twelve hours another service comes on, and, surrounded by the same conditions, his devotions run in the same channel; but he changes his forms of expression, and remembers some things omitted in the former prayer. These services occur twice a day, and erelong he finds his ingenuity at work for a variety of words and thoughts. After a few days, he feels exhausted, and repeats his prayers almost word for word. At this point perhaps Satan tempts him with the thought that his wife and children are tired of his "vain repetitions." He becomes discouraged with his own efforts. His grace fails him. He begins to evade the duty, and directly is openly neglecting it. This condition of things ought not to exist; but it does exist, and perhaps always will exist, among a very large class of parents who really desire to worship God at the family altar, but find the cross greater than they can bear. They see no way to overcome the difficulty, and try to excuse themselves from a duty which they recognize and would be glad to perform. This leads to backsliding, and perhaps to apostasy.

This little book has been prepared for the convenience and assistance of those who feel the need of an "aid and guide" in taking up this important exercise. It contains four services for every morning and evening of a week, each one consisting of a Scripture lesson, a verse or two of song, and a prayer. By this arrangement the same service need not be repeated oftener than once in four weeks. They are all short, requiring not more than from three to five minutes for each one.

In order to have variety, the selections have been made and the prayers have been written by different persons. Those who wrote these prayers were requested to make them simple, earnest, and spiritual, suited to the ordinary occasions of life in a family, and to close them so that they may be supplemented with the Lord's Prayer, or with such additions as may be appropriate to the peculiar conditions of joy or sorrow which often exist, and which properly call for special petitions and thanksgivings.

With such an aid and guide, the mother may conduct the worship in the absence of the father, and the children may be led into a service which will fortify them against the temptations of youth and qualify them for a more responsible period in life.

These forms are not recommended to those who do not need them. Reading them in private may be suggestive to some young Christians who are not familiar with the language of devotion, but who do not approve the use of written prayers. They should be used like a crutch for the lame, or like a support for one learning to swim. They may help the weak until strength comes to go alone. The Ten Commandments, with some parallel passages suitable for family reading on special occasions, are inserted to complete the last form. These parallel selections might be indefinitely increased, but this book is intended for popular use and to be sold at a popular price, and therefore cannot be made larger.

As an humble layman, and with thanks to my brethren of different denominations who have kindly furnished the material here collected together, and with a prayer that these forms may never be read formally, but in the Spirit, this little volume is sent forth with the hope that it may be an instrument under God in establishing many family altars, and in rebuilding many which have been broken down. L. D. PALMER.

SOUTHERN METHODIST PUBLISHING HOUSE,
Nashville, January, 1886.

CONTENTS.

	PAGE
Services for Sunday Morning	7
Sunday Evening	22
Monday Morning	36
Monday Evening	50
Tuesday Morning	62
Tuesday Evening	76
Wednesday Morning	89
Wednesday Evening	100
Thursday Morning	114
Thursday Evening	125
Friday Morning	137
Friday Evening	150
Saturday Morning	162
Saturday Evening	174
Prayer for Opening Sunday-school	185
Prayer for Closing Sunday-school	185
Prayer for Opening Woman's Missionary Meeting	186
Child's Prayer	189
Child's Morning Prayers	189
Child's Evening Prayers	190
The Lord's Prayer	190
Bible Prayers	191
Benedictions	197
Graces Before Meat	200
Graces After Meat	200
The Ten Commandments, with Parallel Readings	201
Scriptural Readings—Covetousness	221
Readings for Special Occasions	224

AID AND GUIDE TO FAMILY WORSHIP.

Services for Sunday Morning.

I. LESSON. 1 John iii. 14–24.

WE know that we have passed from death unto life, because we love the brethren. He that loveth not his brother abideth in death. Whosoever hateth his brother is a murderer; and ye know that no murderer hath eternal life abiding in him. Hereby perceive we the love of God, because he laid down his life for us; and we ought to lay down our lives for the brethren. But whoso hath this world's good, and seeth his brother have need, and shutteth up his bowels of compassion from him, how dwelleth the love of God in him? My little children, let us not love in word, neither in tongue; but in deed and in truth. And hereby we know that we are of the truth, and shall assure our hearts before him. For if our heart condemn us, God is greater than our heart, and knoweth all things. Beloved, if our heart condemn us not, then have we confidence toward God. And whatsoever we ask, we receive of him, because we keep his commandments, and do those things that are pleasing in his sight. And this is his commandment, That we should believe on the name of his Son Jesus Christ, and love one another, as he gave us commandment. And he that keepeth his commandments dwelleth in him, and he in him. And hereby we know that he abideth in us, by the Spirit which he hath given us.

L. M.

Another six days' work is done;
Another Sabbath is begun:
Return, my soul, enjoy thy rest,
Improve the day thy God hath blest.

O that our thoughts and thanks may rise,
As grateful incense, to the skies;
And draw from Christ that sweet repose
Which none but he that feels it knows!

PRAYER.

We praise thee, O Lord, for the return of this day; for the relief it brings to body and mind, the respite it gives from worldly business, its perplexities and temptations; for the quiet it brings to our home, the warmth with which it suffuses our hearts; for the many reunions it secures to parents and children; for the opportunity it offers of going up to the house of

God in company with our loved ones and neighbors; for the instruction it affords through thy ministry, in thy word, and by thy Spirit; and for the gospel of thy grace that is made free to us and to all through the atonement of thy Son and the institution of thy Church. Help us, O God, to manifest our gratitude for these blessings by personally using them; by a fuller self-surrender to thy service; by a heartier coworking with all agents and agencies of good; by a more intimate knowledge of our own wants and the needs of our fellow-men; by a closer sympathy with sinners, and a greater abhorrence of sin itself. And to this end we pray thee to pardon and restore us, to inform us with thy truth, and make us devout by thy Spirit; so that at home and in thy sanctuary we may be ready for any sacrifice, and contribute to the volume of thy praise, the strengthening of thy kingdom in Christian lands and its coming in heathen countries. O holy Father, by thy Spirit qualify our pastor for his office and duty this day, the officers and pupils of the Sunday-school for their work, and get to thyself glory by building up believers in their most holy faith, and by saving the people from their sins; and thine shall be the glory now and forever. Amen.

II. LESSON. <small>Jeremiah xvii. 19–27.</small>

Thus said the Lord unto me: Go and stand in the gate of the children of the people, whereby the kings of Judah come in, and by the which they go out, and in all the gates of Jerusalem; and say unto them, Hear ye the word of the Lord, ye kings of Judah, and all Judah, and all the inhabitants of Jerusalem, that enter in by these gates; thus saith the Lord: Take heed to yourselves, and bear no burden on the Sabbath-day, nor bring it in by the gates of Jerusalem; neither carry forth a burden out of your houses on the Sabbath-day, neither do ye any work, but hallow ye the Sabbath-day, as I commanded your fathers. But they obeyed not, neither inclined their ear, but made their neck stiff, that they might not hear, nor receive instruction. And it shall come to pass, if ye diligently hearken unto me, saith the Lord, to bring in no burden through the gates of this city on the Sabbath-day, but hallow the Sabbath-day, to do no work therein; then shall there enter into the gates of this city kings and princes sitting upon the throne of David, riding in chariots and on horses, they, and their princes, the men of Judah, and the inhabitants of Jerusalem; and this city shall remain forever. And they shall come from the cities of Judah, and from the places about Jerusalem, and from the land of Benjamin, and from the plain and from the mountains, and from the south, bringing burnt-offerings, and sacrifices, and meat-offerings, and incense, and bringing sacrifices of praise, unto the house of the Lord. But if ye will not hearken unto me to hallow the Sabbath-day, and not to bear a burden, even entering in at the gates of Jerusalem on the Sabbath-day; then will I kindle a fire in the gates thereof, and it shall devour the palaces of Jerusalem, and it shall not be quenched.

TRUST in the Lord with all thine heart; and lean not unto thine own understanding. In all thy ways, acknowledge him, and he shall direct thy paths. Honor the Lord with thy substance, and with the first-fruits of all thine increase. So shall thy barns be filled with plenty, and thy presses shall burst out with new wine. My son, despise not the chastening of the Lord; neither be weary of his correction; for whom the Lord loveth he correcteth; even as a father the son in whom he delighteth. Happy is the man that findeth wisdom, and the man that getteth understanding. For the merchandise of it is better than the merchandise of silver, and the gain thereof than fine gold. She is more precious than rubies; and all the things thou canst desire are not to be compared unto her. Length of days is in her right-hand; and in her left-hand riches and honor. Her ways are ways of pleasantness, and all her paths are peace. She is a tree of life to them that lay hold upon her; and happy is every one that retaineth her. Prov. iii. 5, 6, 9–18.

C. M.

This is the day the Lord hath made,
He calls the hours his own;
Let heaven rejoice, let earth be glad,
And praise surround the throne.

PRAYER.

ALMIGHTY GOD, our Heavenly Father, we thank thee for setting apart and sanctifying one day in seven for rest and worship. We gratefully commemorate the resurrection of thy Son, our Saviour, from the dead, whereby he led captivity captive, and brought life and immortality to light. O give us thy quickening Spirit, that we may be prepared for thy worship and praise, both at our homes and in thy house; that the words of our mouths and the meditations of our hearts may be acceptable in thy sight, and that this may be as one of the days of heaven upon earth to our souls. Go with us to thy sanctuary, and make us to realize that thou art in the midst of the congregation. Let thy word be light and life and heavenly news to our hearts and to the hearts of all that shall hear it this day. May thy gospel be attended with convicting and converting power, wherever preached. Make the kingdom of thy Son to prosper in all the earth. Give him the heathen for his inheritance and the uttermost parts of the earth for his possession. Give power and prevalence to thy Church, and make the nations to know themselves to be but men. May we remember this thy day to keep it holy. Teach us to examine ourselves and turn from every sinful way. Forgive our sins, and help us to walk in the future more worthy of our high vocation. Suit thy blessings to our personal needs; prepare us to sympathize with the distressed, to aid the needy, and at all times to do and suffer thy will. Hear us in behalf of the sick and the suffering. Give peace to the troubled soul, and graciously pardon the penitent sinner. May all thy children be faithful, and constantly grow in grace. Hasten the spread of thy kingdom till it shall fill the whole earth. Empower us each to do our part, and help us to be faithful unto death, that we may receive the crown of life. Amen.

III. LESSON. Mark xvi. 1-16.

AND when the Sabbath was past, Mary Magdalene, and Mary the mother of James, and Salome, had bought sweet spices, that they might come and anoint him. And very early in the morning, the first day of the week, they came unto the sepulcher at the rising of the sun. And they said among themselves, Who shall roll us away the stone from the door of the sepulcher? And when they looked, they saw that the stone was rolled away; for it was very great. And entering into the sepulcher, they saw a young man sitting on the right side, clothed in a long white garment; and they were affrighted. And he saith unto them, Be not affrighted; ye seek Jesus of Nazareth, which was crucified; he is risen; he is not here; behold the place where they laid him. But go your way, tell his disciples and Peter, that he goeth before you into Galilee; there shall ye see him, as he said unto you. And they went out quickly, and fled from the sepulcher; for they trembled, and were amazed; neither said they any thing to any man; for they were afraid. Now when Jesus was risen early, the first day of the week, he appeared first to Mary Magdalene, out of whom he had cast seven devils. And she went and told them that had been with him, as they mourned and wept. And they, when they had heard that he was alive, and had been seen of her, believed not. After that, he appeared in another form unto two of them, as they walked, and went into the country. And they went and told it unto the residue; neither believed they them. Afterward he appeared unto the eleven, as they sat at meat, and upbraided them with their unbelief, and hardness of heart, because they believed not them which had seen him after he was risen. And he said unto them, Go ye into all the world, and preach the gospel to every creature. He that believeth and is baptized, shall be saved; but he that believeth not, shall be damned.

10, 9.

We would praise thee and bless thee, our Father,
  For the Sabbath of rest thou hast given;
'T is the emblem of rapture immortal,
'T is the foretaste of pleasure in heaven.

Refrain: Sweet Sabbath of rest, sweet Sabbath of rest!
    Sweet, sweet rest!
  We would laud thee and thank thee, our Father,
    For the gift of this Sabbath of rest.

PRAYER.

O LORD, our Heavenly Father, we praise thee for the privilege of calling thee our Father, and would realize that we are indeed thy children. Thy parental care has been over us through the duties, toils, and vicissitudes of another week. Thy goodness has followed us every moment, and thy mercy attended every step. O give us hearts of gratitude this morning for all these thy favors conferred upon us. Poor, unworthy creatures, may we not only express our gratitude with our lips, but may we, as dutiful and appreciative children, honor thee, our gracious Father, by the deepest feelings of our hearts and the undivided service of our lives. This blessed day brings to us special privileges and duties. O God, our Heavenly Father, prepare us, by the influence of the Holy Spirit, to improve its privileges and perform its duties. O may the hearts of thy people everywhere leap for joy in contemplating the great blessings of this hallowed day, the first day of the week, when Christ arose from the dead, and gave to a dying world the hope of everlasting life. O may thine earthly courts everywhere be crowded to-day with anxious multitudes worshiping thee in spirit and in truth. O Lord, hasten the day when all the people shall say, "I was glad when they said unto me, Let us go up to the house of the Lord to-day." Pour thy Spirit upon all congregations that meet to worship in thy name to-day. Bless every soul that worships thee in sincerity. Fill all thy people with love to thee and one another. Bless all who minister before thee to-day with all the fullness of an unction from on high. Grant that their words may be powerful words, through thy power, sanctifying thy people and converting sinners. O Lord, help us to spend this Sabbath-day in reference to that one that shall have no end. And may we so worship together here, and so live, that we may all meet in that congregation that shall never break up. Now, Lord, hear our poor prayers, forgive our sins, bless our souls, and save us with the power of an endless life, through riches of grace in Christ Jesus. Amen.

IV. LESSON. Mark ii. 23-28.

AND it came to pass, that he went through the corn-fields on the Sabbath-day; and his disciples began, as they went, to pluck the ears of corn. And the Pharisees said unto him, Behold, why do they on the Sabbath-day that which is not lawful? And he said unto them, Have ye never read what David did, when he had need, and was a-hungered, he, and they that were with him? how he went into the house of God in the days of Abiathar the high-priest, and did eat the shew-bread, which is not lawful to eat but for the priests, and gave also to them which were with him? And he said unto them, The Sabbath was made for man, and not man for the Sabbath; therefore the Son of man is Lord also of the Sabbath. ———

LORD, who shall abide in thy tabernacle? who shall dwell in thy holy hill? He that walketh uprightly, and worketh righteousness, and speaketh the truth in his heart. He that backbiteth not with his tongue, nor doeth evil to his neighbor, nor taketh up a reproach against his neighbor. In whose eyes a vile person is contemned; but he honoreth them that fear the Lord. He that sweareth to his own hurt, and changeth not. He that putteth not out his money to usury, nor taketh reward against the innocent. He that doeth these things shall never be moved. **Psalm xv.**

L. M.

THINE earthly Sabbaths, Lord, we love;
But there's a nobler rest above;
To that our lab'ring souls aspire,
With ardent pangs of strong desire.

PRAYER.

We thank thee, O Lord, that we are spared to see the light of this thy holy day, with health and reason and desire to worship thee. We present ourselves before thee, as we enter on the day, to offer thee our Sunday morning's sacrifice of praise and prayer through Jesus Christ our Lord. For his sake, we pray thee, accept our praises, hear our prayers, forgive our sins, and bless and sanctify and save our sin-sick souls. Grant us thy grace, that we may use this day to profit; that we may learn to love thee more and serve thee better; that we may make a full day's journey toward our heavenly home. If we attend the public preaching of thy word, may we be blessed in listening to the message of thy truth, and may the Holy Ghost apply the word to all our hearts, and make us wise unto salvation. Bless all thy servants who may stand this day to publish to their fellow-men the gospel of thy grace. May thy word have free course, and be glorified in the conviction of sinners, in the comfort of those who seek thee sorrowing, and in the building up of thy people on their most holy faith. May many be induced to-day to turn away from sin, and come to thee for mercy; and may thy people everywhere be furthered in the way which leads to everlasting life. Especially be with those whom thou hast sent to distant lands to preach the gospel to the heathen. May they this day be all encouraged in their work, by seeing men renounce their idols and embrace the worship of our Saviour Jesus Christ. And do thou speed the happy day when thou wilt give the heathen to thy Son for his inheritance, and the uttermost parts of the earth for his possession. And O employ each one of us in spreading thy kingdom in the earth. Smile with especial tenderness upon the children of the Church and of the world at large. Give to all parents true views of their duty and their privilege; and enable and induce them, by precept and example, to bring up their children in thy nurture and admonition. Bless the Sunday-school cause. Give zeal and wisdom to all those in charge of the spiritual training of the young, and give them eminent success in inducing the children to engage in thy service in the days of their youth. Thus may those soon to come upon the stage of active life be better fitted and disposed for all their duties than those who occupy it now; and may the world soon reach the blissful time when every knee shall bow and every tongue confess that

Jesus Christ is Lord, to thy glory as the all-Father. And now, O Heavenly King, look with tender interest upon all thine earthly creatures. Be merciful to the sick, the poor, and all who are distressed in any way. Bless all our friends; and do thou good to those who do us harm; and let us live in peace with all mankind, so that our earthly lives may be a constant foretaste of the heavenly Sabbath which shall have no end. And when we reach our happy home above, the praise of our salvation shall be ever thine, through Jesus Christ the Lord. Amen.

The Lord is my shepherd; I shall not want. He maketh me to lie down in green pastures; he leadeth me beside the still waters. He restoreth my soul; he leadeth me in the paths of righteousness for his name's sake. Yea, though I walk through the valley of the shadow of death, I will fear no evil; for thou art with me; thy rod and thy staff they comfort me. Thou preparest a table before me in the presence of mine enemies; thou anointest my head with oil; my cup runneth over. Surely goodness and mercy shall follow me all the days of my life; and I will dwell in the house of the Lord forever. *Psalm xxiii.*

Services for Sunday Evening.

I. LESSON. Psalm xci.

He that dwelleth in the secret place of the Most High shall abide under the shadow of the Almighty. I will say of the Lord, He is my refuge and my fortress; my God; in him will I trust. Surely he shall deliver thee from the snare of the fowler, and from the noisome pestilence. He shall cover thee with his feathers, and under his wings shalt thou trust; his truth shall be thy shield and buckler. Thou shalt not be afraid for the terror by night; nor for the arrow that flieth by day; nor for the pestilence that walketh in darkness; nor for the destruction that wasteth at noonday. A thousand shall fall at thy side, and ten thousand at thy right-hand; but it shall not come nigh thee. Only with thine eyes shalt thou behold and see the reward of the wicked. Because thou hast made the Lord, which is my refuge, even the Most High, thy habitation; there shall no evil befall thee, neither shall any plague come nigh thy dwelling. For he shall give his angels charge over thee, to keep thee in all thy ways. They shall bear thee up in their hands, lest thou dash thy foot against a stone. Thou shalt tread upon the lion and adder: the young lion and the dragon shalt thou trample under feet. Because he hath set his love upon me, therefore will I deliver him: I will set him on high, because he hath known my name. He shall call upon me, and I will answer him: I will be with him in trouble; I will deliver him, and honor him. With long life will I satisfy him, and show him my salvation.

Thus saith the Lord, Keep ye judgment, and do justice; for my salvation is near to come, and my righteousness to be revealed. Blessed is the man that doeth this, and the son of man that layeth hold on it; that keepeth the Sabbath from polluting it, and keepeth his hand from doing any evil. Isaiah lvi. 1, 2.

S. M.

The power to bless my house
  Belongs to God alone;
Yet, rend'ring him my constant vows,
  He sends his blessings down.
Shall I not then engage
  My house to serve the Lord,
To search the soul-converting page,
  And feed upon his word?

PRAYER.

O LORD, our God, excellent is thy name in all the earth. We would give thee humble and sincere thanks for all the blessings of this day. Thou hast blessed our going out and our coming in. O fill our hearts with gratitude for all thy mercies, and with penitence for all our sins. May the remembrance of our short-comings and misdoings be grievous unto us; and may we by the guidance of thy word and the aid of thy Spirit turn from all unrighteousness. Help us to love thee with all our heart, and serve thee with all our strength. We confess and lament our unfaithfulness before thee. Increase our faith, O Lord, and so warm our hearts by a sense of thy love shed abroad therein that we may more devoutly worship and more earnestly serve thee all our days. We mourn over the hardness of our hearts, the waywardness of our lives, and the inconstancy of our zeal. Help thou the infirmities of our fallen natures, and strengthen us for every good word and work. We would humbly serve thy purpose in creating us and placing us in the world. Prepare us to do and suffer thy will with cheerfulness and patience. Bring the best results from all that we have striven to do; and bless us in our earthly fortunes and in our hopes of heaven. Let thy kingdom come in all the earth, and move us to do our duty in bringing men to Christ. Preserve us from all harm this night; refresh us with sleep; be with us when we wake, and guide us through this life unto everlasting life in heaven, for Christ's sake. Amen.

II. LESSON. Hebrews xii. 18-29.

For ye are not come unto the mount that might be touched, and that burned with fire, nor unto blackness, and darkness, and tempest, and the sound of a trumpet, and the voice of words; which voice they that heard entreated that the word should not be spoken to them any more (for they could not endure that which was commanded: And if so much as a beast touch the mountain, it shall be stoned, or thrust through with a dart; and so terrible was the sight, that Moses said, I exceedingly fear and quake); but ye are come unto mount Sion, and unto the city of the living God, the heavenly Jerusalem, and to an innumerable company of angels, to the general assembly and church of the first-born, which are written in heaven, and to God the Judge of all, and to the spirits of just men made perfect, and to Jesus the Mediator of the new covenant, and to the blood of sprinkling, that speaketh better things than that of Abel. See that ye refuse not him that speaketh; for if they escaped not who refused him that spake on earth, much more shall not we escape, if we turn away from him that speaketh from heaven; whose voice then shook the earth; but now he hath promised, saying, Yet once more I shake not the earth only, but also heaven. And this word, Yet once more, signifieth the removing of those things that are shaken, as of things that are made, that those things which cannot be shaken may remain. Wherefore we receiving a kingdom which cannot be moved, let us have grace, whereby we may serve God acceptably with reverence and godly fear; for our God is a consuming fire.

C. M.

Come, let us who in Christ believe,
  Our common Saviour praise:
To him, with joyful voices, give
  The glory of his grace.
Through grace we hearken to thy voice,
  Yield to be saved from sin;
In sure and certain hope rejoice,
  That thou wilt enter in.

PRAYER.

We thank thee, O Lord, for the holy Sabbath, so full of blessings for thy children. We adore thee for this memorial of the precious work of our redemption, and type of the rest that remains for the people of God. Help us to keep the day holy. May we be richly blessed in reading thy word, in listening to thy gospel, and in all the services of the holy day. Be with all ministers of the gospel, and especially with those who have preached thy word to-day. Bless our children, at home and in the Sabbath-school. Give to the teachers the power to mold character and to guide the children along the path of the just. Comfort all that mourn, especially such as have not been allowed to attend thy house on this thy holy day. Give us grace not merely to hear the word, but to help in the spread of light and life over the world. Make us spiritual. Fill us with gratitude. Enable us to live nearer to thee. May each Sabbath be a spiritual benediction to all thy people. Look upon those who are yet sitting in darkness and in the shadow of death. Send abroad thy light and thy truth into the benighted portions of our globe. Turn the nations from idols to serve the living God. Let the people praise thee, let all the people praise thee; and blessed be thy glorious name forever and ever. Amen.

III. LESSON. Isaiah lv. 1-11.

Ho, every one that thirsteth, come ye to the waters, and he that hath no money, come ye, buy, and eat; yea, come, buy wine and milk without money and without price. Wherefore do ye spend money for that which is not bread? and your labor for that which satisfieth not? hearken diligently unto me, and eat ye that which is good, and let your soul delight itself in fatness. Incline your ear, and come unto me; hear, and your soul shall live; and I will make an everlasting covenant with you, even the sure mercies of David. Behold, I have given him for a witness to the people, a leader and commander to the people. Behold, thou shalt call a nation that thou knowest not, and nations that knew not thee shall run unto thee, because of the Lord thy God, and for the Holy One of Israel; for he hath glorified thee. Seek ye the Lord while he may be found, call ye upon him while he is near; let the wicked forsake his way, and the unrighteous man his thoughts; and let him return unto the Lord, and he will have mercy upon him; and to our God, for he will abundantly pardon. For my thoughts are not your thoughts, neither are your ways my ways, saith the Lord. For as the heavens are higher than the earth, so are my ways higher than your ways, and my thoughts than your thoughts. For as the rain cometh down, and the snow from heaven, and returneth not thither, but watereth the earth, and maketh it bring forth and bud, that it may give seed to the sower, and bread to the eater: so shall my word be that goeth forth out of my mouth; it shall not return unto me void, but it shall accomplish that which I please, and it shall prosper in the thing whereto I sent it.

A soft answer turneth away wrath; but grievous words stir up anger. The eyes of the Lord are in every place, beholding the evil and the good. Better is little with the fear of the Lord than great treasure and trouble therewith. The Lord is far from the wicked; but he heareth the prayer of the righteous.

Proverbs xv. 1, 3, 16, 29.

11 s.

How firm a foundation, ye saints of the Lord,
Is laid for your faith in his excellent word!
What more can he say than to you he hath said,
You who unto Jesus for refuge have fled?

"The soul that on Jesus still leans for repose,
I *will* not, I *will* not, desert to his foes;
That soul, though all hell should endeavor to shake,
I'll never, *no, never*, NO, NEVER forsake."

PRAYER.

We give thee praise, holy Father, for this thy day. We would honor and magnify thy great and glorious name for the gift of this precious day, and all the holy privileges which attended its coming, and which we have enjoyed. We feel our unworthiness to take upon our lips thy great name, and the coming of thy blessed Sabbath renews our sense of unworthiness and impurity. We dare not approach thy name or thy day in our own strength, but in the name and strength of our Lord Jesus Christ we have ventured into thy presence and worshiped thy matchless name, and have endeavored to remember the Sabbath-day to keep it holy. Wherein we have failed in these duties, O Lord, grant us full forgiveness for the sake of thy blessed Son. Put thy Spirit, blessed Father, upon the seed thy servants have this day sown. May they have spoken as the oracles of God, and may thy word run and be glorified, and accomplish that whereto thou hast sent it. May the sorrowing and bereaved be comforted, and souls be saved from sin and death, by the ministrations of thy servants. And now, in meekness of spirit, with love unfeigned and with child-like faith, may we commit all we have and are into thy hands. Protect us during the hours of sleep. Keep far from us all danger. And may we be refreshed and strengthened by the rest of the night for the duties of the coming day. Grant this, we beseech thee, for the sake of thy Son our Saviour Jesus Christ. Amen.

IV. LESSON. Gen. xxviii. 10–22.

AND Jacob went out from Beer-sheba, and went toward Haran. And he lighted upon a certain place, and tarried there all night, because the sun was set; and he took of the stones of that place, and put them for his pillows, and lay down in that place to sleep. And he dreamed, and behold, a ladder set up on the earth, and the top of it reached to heaven; and behold, the angels of God ascending and descending on it. And behold, the Lord stood above it, and said, I am the Lord God of Abraham thy father, and the God of Isaac; the land whereon thou liest, to thee will I give it, and to thy seed; and thy seed shall be as the dust of the earth; and thou shalt spread abroad to the west, and to the east, and to the north, and to the south; and in thee and in thy seed shall all the families of the earth be blessed. And behold, I am with thee, and will keep thee in all places whither thou goest, and will bring thee again into this land; for I will not leave thee, until I have done that which I have spoken to thee of. And Jacob awaked out of his sleep, and he said, Surely the Lord is in this place; and I knew it not. And he was afraid, and said, How dreadful is this place! this is none other but the house of God, and this is the gate of heaven. And Jacob rose up early in the morning, and took the stone that he had put for his pillows, and set it up for a pillar, and poured oil upon the top of it. And he called the name of that place Bethel; but the name of that city was called Luz at the first. And Jacob vowed a vow, saying, If God will be with me, and will keep me in this way that I go, and will give me bread to eat, and raiment to put on, so that I come again to my father's house in peace; then shall the Lord be my God; and this stone, which I have set for a pillar, shall be God's house; and of all that thou shalt give me, I will surely give the tenth unto thee.

L. M.

This, this is the God we adore,
  Our faithful, unchangeable Friend,
Whose love is as great as his power,
  And neither knows measure nor end.

PRAYER.

We come before thee, Heavenly Father, at the close of the Sabbath-day, to thank thee for allowing us one day in seven to rest our bodies and our minds from worldly labor, and to lean our spirits specially on thee, our Father and our God. We bless thee for thy Holy Word, with all its precious lessons of divine instruction, designed to guide us in the way which leads from earth to heaven. We adore thee for the Christian Church, for the means of grace, and for the hope of glory which fills our hearts to-night. We worship thee that thou hast sent the Holy Ghost, the Comforter, to impress upon our souls the lessons of thy word, to stir our consciences to do their work, and to assure us of our adoption into the family above. All these and all thy other mercies come to us through Jesus Christ, thy Son, our Lord, through whom we offer thee our homage now and evermore. Fill us with gratitude to thee, and grant that we may show our love, not with our lips alone, but in our daily lives. May this day's privileges make us wiser, humbler, purer, better than we were before. May we hereafter love thee more and serve thee better than we have ever done; and may we love each other also, and our neighbors too, with purer and more ardent affection. May we delight in doing good to others in every way, but especially in inducing them to devote themselves to thee. O make us instruments in extending thy kingdom, and blessing and saving our dying fellowmen. Look tenderly, O Lord, on all thy servants who are striving to extend the borders of thy Zion. Wherever this day the good seed of the kingdom has been sown, in mercy send the sunshine of thy love, and showers of grace divine, that it may spring up and bring forth fruit to thy glory, in the welfare and salvation of the people. Be very gracious unto all who have to-day been made to feel their lost condition and to long for freedom from the slavery of sin. May they find no rest until they turn away from all their wickedness, and humbly trust the precious merits of our Saviour Jesus Christ. And unto all who seek thee sorrowing appear in all thy loveliness, and let them feel the kindlings of thy love and the joys of thy great salvation. Remember still in tender pity those who have resisted all thy merciful appeals, and seem determined to persist in sin until they bring themselves to ruin. Leave them not, O gracious Father, to themselves; but by thy Spirit and thy Word, by dealings of thy providence, both pleasant and severe, by efforts of their pious fellow-men, or by such other means as it may please thee to adopt, continue unto them the offer of salvation, if perchance they may repent of their misdeeds, and turn to thee, and live. We now commend to thy protecting care ourselves and all for whom we ought to pray. Throughout the watches of the night defend our absent dear ones from every evil thing. Let no alarm of fire, or serious sickness, or sudden death invade their homes; but may they rest safe and secure within thy hollow hand; and, rising in the morning, go about their work, to spend the strength thou givest them in serving thee. May they and we be guided by thy counsels through the pilgrimage of life, and receive at last an entrance abundantly into the everlasting kingdom of our Lord and Saviour Jesus Christ. Amen.

EVEN so every good tree bringeth forth good fruit, but a corrupt tree bringeth forth evil fruit. A good tree cannot bring forth evil fruit, neither can a corrupt tree bring forth good fruit. Every tree that bringeth not forth good fruit is hewn down, and cast into the fire. Wherefore by their fruits ye shall know them. Matthew vii, 17-20.

Services for Monday Morning.

I. LESSON.   Romans xii. 9-21.

LET love be without dissimulation. Abhor that which is evil; cleave to that which is good. Be kindly affectioned one to another with brotherly love; in honor preferring one another; not slothful in business; fervent in spirit; serving the Lord; rejoicing in hope; patient in tribulation; continuing instant in prayer; distributing to the necessity of saints; given to hospitality. Bless them which persecute you; bless, and curse not. Rejoice with them that do rejoice, and weep with them that weep. Be of the same mind one toward another. Mind not high things, but condescend to men of low estate. Be not wise in your own conceits. Recompense to no man evil for evil. Provide things honest in the sight of all men. If it be possible, as much as lieth in you, live peaceably with all men. Dearly beloved, avenge not yourselves, but rather give place unto wrath; for it is written, Vengeance is mine; I will repay, saith the Lord. Therefore if thine enemy hunger, feed him; if he thirst, give him drink; for in so doing thou shalt heap coals of fire on his head. Be not overcome of evil, but overcome evil with good.

O Lord our Lord, how excellent is thy name in all the earth! who hast set thy glory above the heavens. Out of the mouth of babes and sucklings hast thou ordained strength because of thine enemies, that thou mightest still the enemy and the avenger. When I consider thy heavens, the work of thy fingers, the moon and the stars, which thou hast ordained; what is man, that thou art mindful of him? and the son of man, that thou visitest him? for thou hast made him a little lower than the angels, and hast crowned him with glory and honor. Thou madest him to have dominion over the works of thy hands; thou hast put all things under his feet; all sheep and oxen, yea, and the beasts of the field; the fowl of the air, and the fish of the sea, and whatsoever passeth through the paths of the seas. O Lord our Lord, how excellent is thy name in all the earth!

Psalm viii.

C. M.

When all thy mercies, O my God,
  My rising soul surveys,
Transported with the view, I'm lost
  In wonder, love, and praise!

O how can words with equal warmth
  The gratitude declare
That glows within my ravished heart?
  But thou canst read it there!

PRAYER.

WE thank thee, Father, for the refreshing sleep and the felt security of the past night; for the health of body and soul we enjoy; for the hopes of usefulness and happiness that inspire and the Christian faith that sustains us. Lead us, we pray thee, to godly repentance for any want of filial love or obedience, any willful breaking of thy law, of which we may be guilty; and assure us, by the Holy Spirit, of our forgiveness and of thy continued favor. As the Father of this family as well as of the whole family "in heaven and earth," we would take counsel of thee for this day's work. Suggest to us the wisest plans; save us from errors of judgment; stimulate us to diligence, and yet deliver us from a mere selfish industry; help us to look on the things of others as well as upon our own; and above all, cause us to be momently conscious of thy approval. Make our home busy in good works and beautiful in blessed charities. May a cheerful sanctity characterize us here and wherever duty may place us. As parents, may we be holy and discreet; as children, dutiful and docile; as servants, faithful and obedient. Bless each and all of us in such manner that we shall be kept from sin and furthered in the knowledge and grace of thy Son our Saviour, the Lord Jesus Christ. Amen.

II. LESSON. Psalm xxxvii. 1-11.

FRET not thyself because of evil-doers, neither be thou envious against the workers of iniquity. For they shall soon be cut down like the grass, and wither as the green herb. Trust in the Lord, and do good; so shalt thou dwell in the land, and verily thou shalt be fed. Delight thyself also in the Lord; and he shall give thee the desires of thine heart. Commit thy way unto the Lord; trust also in him; and he shall bring it to pass. And he shall bring forth thy righteousness as the light, and thy judgment as the noonday. Rest in the Lord, and wait patiently for him; fret not thyself because of him who prospereth in his way, because of the man who bringeth wicked devices to pass. Cease from anger, and forsake wrath; fret not thyself in any wise to do evil. For evil-doers shall be cut off; but those that wait upon the Lord, they shall inherit the earth. For yet a little while, and the wicked shall not be; yea, thou shalt diligently consider his place, and it shall not be. But the meek shall inherit the earth; and shall delight themselves in the abundance of peace.

KEEP me as the apple of the eye; hide me under the shadow of thy wings. Psalm xvii. 8.

L. M.

Forth in thy name, O Lord, I go,
 My daily labor to pursue;
Thee, only thee, resolved to know
 In all I think, or speak, or do.

Thee may I set at my right-hand,
 Whose eyes my inmost substance see;
And labor on at thy command,
 And offer all my works to thee.

PRAYER.

Our Heavenly Father, we come this morning to renew our expressions of gratitude to thee for thy continued goodness and mercy to us. We thank thee, we trust from the depths of our hearts, for the repose of the night whereby our bodies have been refreshed, and our minds temporarily relieved from anxious cares, and both the spiritual and physical man the better prepared for the business and duties of another day. And now, Lord, as the duties, obligations, and it may be dangers, of this new day are upon us, we humbly pray the guidance of the Holy Spirit in all things. Grant us grace for all the duties, trials, and obligations of the day. May we take our religion into every business transaction of this day, and thereby convince every one with whom we come in contact of the reality of our profession, and that we are deeply in earnest about doing right and getting to heaven. O forgive us our sins, and keep us from doing wrong today. May we not engage in any thing upon which we may not in confidence ask thy blessing. And may we always remember, O Lord, that the ability to keep thy commandments and do thy will comes from thee. And as thou hast instructed us by thy servant to commit our ways unto thee, and promised to direct our paths, so we pray thee, our Heavenly Father, for the sake of Jesus our dear Saviour, to direct us always in the way in which we should go, and help us continue therein to the final end. Then, when life's toils are over, give us the Christian's triumph in death, and in heaven's beautiful land, where it will be so "sweet to meet one another again," save us all, for Christ our Redeemer's sake. Amen.

BE not deceived; God is not mocked; for whatsoever a man soweth, that shall he also reap. For he that soweth to his flesh shall of the flesh reap corruption; but he that soweth to the Spirit shall of the Spirit reap life everlasting. And let us not be weary in well-doing, for in due season we shall reap, if we faint not.
Galatians vi. 7-9.

III. LESSON. 1 Corinthians xiii.

Though I speak with the tongues of men and of angels, and have not charity, I am become as sounding brass, or a tinkling cymbal. And though I have the gift of prophecy, and understand all mysteries, and all knowledge; and though I have all faith, so that I could remove mountains, and have not charity, I am nothing. And though I bestow all my goods to feed the poor, and though I give my body to be burned, and have not charity, it profiteth me nothing. Charity suffereth long, and is kind; charity envieth not; charity vaunteth not itself, is not puffed up, doth not behave itself unseemly, seeketh not her own, is not easily provoked, thinketh no evil; rejoiceth not in iniquity, but rejoiceth in the truth; beareth all things, believeth all things, hopeth all things, endureth all things. Charity never faileth; but whether there be prophecies, they shall fail; whether there be tongues, they shall cease; whether there be knowledge, it shall vanish away. For we know in part, and we prophesy in part. But when that which is perfect is come, then that which is in part shall be done away. When I was a child, I spake as a child, I understood as a child, I thought as a child; but when I became a man, I put away childish things. For now we see through a glass, darkly; but then face to face; now I know in part; but then shall I know even as also I am known. And now abideth faith, hope, charity, these three; but the greatest of these is charity.

WISDOM is the principal thing; therefore get wisdom; and with all thy getting get understanding. Exalt her, and she shall promote thee; she shall bring thee to honor, when thou dost embrace her. But the path of the just is as the shining light, that shineth more and more unto the perfect day. The way of the wicked is as darkness; they know not at what they stumble. Keep thy heart with all diligence; for out of it are the issues of life. Put away from thee a froward mouth, and perverse lips put far from thee. Proverbs iv. 7, 8, 18, 19, 23, 24.

L. M. No. 951, Hymn-book.

AWAKE, my soul, and with the sun
Thy daily stage of duty run;
Shake off dull sloth, and early rise
To pay thy morning sacrifice.

Glory to Thee, who safe hast kept,
And hast refreshed me while I slept:
Grant, Lord, when I from death shall wake,
I may of endless life partake.

PRAYER.

ALMIGHTY and everlasting God, thou art the author, preserver, and benefactor of our lives; and we esteem it a good thing to give thanks unto thee, to show forth thy loving-kindness every morning and thy faithfulness every night. Especially are we called upon at this time to recognize thy providential favor through the past night. For our preservation from danger, disease, and death; for the refreshment derived from sleep; and for all the opening mercies of another day, we render thee devout and hearty thanks. We acknowledge ourselves wholly unworthy of the least of all thy mercies, for we have sinned and come short of thy glory. But we rejoice that thy Son, Jesus Christ, was manifested to take away our sins. Through his name, in humble dependence upon his merits, we approach thee, imploring forgiveness for all past offenses, and grace whereby for the time to come we may serve thee acceptably, with reverence and godly fear, in holiness and righteousness, all the days of our lives. Let thy blessing be upon us this day. Preserve us from all temporal and spiritual harm. Strengthen us for the resistance of every temptation and the performance of every duty. We know not what a day may bring forth. Prepare us for whatever thy providence may appoint. In all the changing scenes of life may we trustfully recognize thy hand and patiently submit to thy holy will, saying: "It is the Lord; let him do as seemeth him good." Bless us as a family. Unite us, not only in the bonds of natural affection, but in the faith and fellowship and hope of the gospel. Regard with thy special favor our dear kindred and friends. Do for them exceedingly abundantly above all that we can either ask or think. Be very merciful to those who are in affliction and trouble. May the wants of the needy be supplied. Comfort the sorrowing. Heal the sick, or prepare them for approaching death. Look compassionately upon those who are yet strangers to thee. Bring all men everywhere to a knowledge of thyself, the only true God, and Jesus Christ, whom thou hast sent. All of which we ask in the name of Christ, our adorable Redeemer. Amen.

Seest thou a man wise in his own conceit? there is more hope of a fool than of him. Where no wood is, there the fire goeth out; so where there is no tale-bearer, the strife ceaseth. Proverbs xxvi. 12, 20.

IV. LESSON. Philippians ii. 1–16.

If there be therefore any consolation in Christ, if any comfort of love, if any fellowship of the Spirit, if any bowels and mercies, fulfill ye my joy, that ye be like-minded, having the same love, being of one accord, of one mind. Let nothing be done through strife or vainglory; but in lowliness of mind let each esteem other better than themselves. Look not every man on his own things, but every man also on the things of others. Let this mind be in you, which was also in Christ Jesus; who, being in the form of God, thought it not robbery to be equal with God; but made himself of no reputation, and took upon him the form of a servant, and was made in the likeness of men; and being found in fashion as a man, he humbled himself, and became obedient unto death, even the death of the cross. Wherefore God also hath highly exalted him, and given him a name which is above every name; that at the name of Jesus every knee should bow, of things in heaven, and things in earth, and things under the earth; and that every tongue should confess that Jesus Christ is Lord, to the glory of God the Father. Wherefore, my beloved, as ye have always obeyed, not as in my presence only, but now much more in my absence, work out your own salvation with fear and trembling; for it is God which worketh in you both to will and to do of his good pleasure. Do all things without murmurings and disputings; that ye may be blameless and harmless, the sons of God, without rebuke, in the midst of a crooked and perverse nation, among whom ye shine as lights in the world; holding forth the word of life; that I may rejoice in the day of Christ, that I have not run in vain, neither labored in vain.

73.

Loving Jesus, gentle Lamb,
In thy gracious hands I am:
Make me, Saviour, what thou art,
Live thyself within my heart.

I shall then show forth thy praise,
Serve thee all my happy days,
Then the world shall always see
Christ, the holy Child, in me.

PRAYER.

Spared by thy mercy through the night, we come together now, O Lord, to bring to thee our Monday morning's offering of prayer and praise through Jesus Christ our Saviour. For his sake, grant us now the Holy Spirit, to quicken our gratitude and to inspire our prayers, that our devotions may be acceptable to thee, and result in blessings large and free to every one of us. For his sake accept our thanks for all the mercies of the night and for the benefits and blessings which have fallen to our lot from infancy till now. Surely thy goodness and mercy have followed us all the days of our lives; and we would show forth our gratitude to thee by walking in constant obedience to thy holy laws. Impress us afresh this morning with the great value of the Christian Sabbath, and with the debt of gratitude we owe thee for giving us its benefits again. May the spirit of the holy day be with each one of us in all the labors and business of the week on which we enter; so that, whether we eat or drink, or whatsoever we do, we may do all to the glory of thy name. Enable us to feel that we are not our own, but that we are bought with a price, and that we should therefore glorify thee in our bodies and in our spirits, which are thine. We know not what this day may bring forth. We pray thee to prepare us for all that may befall us as it passes by. Without thy help and blessing, we can not prosper in any thing. Give us such success in all our proper efforts as may be best for us and most conducive to thy glory; and, if it please thee to blast our highest hopes, give us a spirit of submission to thy will, and satisfaction that thou doest for us all things well. May we not look for highest happiness from earthly objects or pursuits; but, ever mindful of our heavenly origin and destiny, may we regard thee as the only source of pure and perfect bliss. Confine not thy blessings, Heavenly Father, unto us. Smile graciously on all who are connected with us by the ties of kindred or the cords of love. May all their interests for this life and the life to come be precious in thy sight, and may they all devote themselves to thee. We pray for those who are confined this day to beds of sickness, unable to engage in the duties of active life. Give them patience in their affliction; and, if it please thee, restore them soon to health and soundness. Command thy blessing, Heavenly Teacher, source of all true wisdom, upon all instructors of youth and all young persons at school, that, through their mutual labors, the cause of sanctified learning may be advanced, and ignorance and vice be driven from our land. And now, O Father, our prayer is before thee. Hear us and bless us, and sanctify and save us; for all we ask is in the precious name of Jesus Christ the Lord. Amen.

Services for Monday Evening.

I. LESSON.   1 Peter v. 1-11.

The elders which are among you I exhort, who am also an elder, and a witness of the sufferings of Christ, and also a partaker of the glory that shall be revealed: feed the flock of God which is among you, taking the oversight thereof, not by constraint, but willingly; not for filthy lucre, but of a ready mind; neither as being lords over God's heritage, but being ensamples to the flock. And when the chief Shepherd shall appear, ye shall receive a crown of glory that fadeth not away. Likewise, ye younger, submit yourselves unto the elder. Yea, all of you be subject one to another, and be clothed with humility; for God resisteth the proud, and giveth grace to the humble. Humble yourselves therefore under the mighty hand of God, that he may exhalt you in due time; casting all your care upon him; for he careth for you. Be sober, be vigilant; because your adversary the devil, as a roaring lion, walketh about, seeking whom he may devour: whom resist steadfast in the faith, knowing that the same afflictions are accomplished in your brethren that are in the world. But the God of all grace, who hath called us unto his eternal glory by Christ Jesus, after that ye have suffered awhile, make you perfect, stablish, strengthen, settle you. To him be glory and dominion forever and ever. Amen.

Ask, and it shall be given you; seek, and ye shall find; knock, and it shall be opened unto you; for every one that asketh receiveth; and he that seeketh findeth; and to him that knocketh it shall be opened. Or what man is there of you, whom if his son ask bread, will he give him a stone? or if he ask a fish, will he give him a serpent? If ye then, being evil, know how to give good gifts unto your children, how much more shall your Father which is in heaven give good things to them that ask him? Therefore all things whatsoever ye would that men should do to you, do ye even so to them; for this is the law and the prophets.

Matthew vi. 7-12.

C. M.

Now from the altar of our hearts
  Let warmest thanks arise;
Assist us, Lord, to offer up
  Our evening sacrifice.

This day God was our sun and shield,
  Our keeper and our guide;
His care was on our weakness shown,
  His mercies multiplied.

PRAYER.

WE thank thee, our loving Creator, for the institution of the family, for the beautiful relations of husband and wife, parents and children. We thank thee for our home, with all its comforts and blessings. We pray thee, O Father, make our home a model of Christian virtues: let love, pure and sweet, bind heart to heart; let mutual confidence reign in our midst; make us a harmonious, happy Christian family. Bring us closer to thee and closer to each other. Give to us as parents, gentleness and firmness, that we may properly rule our household. Give to our dear children love for each other, and help them to be both loving and obedient to their parents. Save us from sickness and all overwhelming calamities. Bless dear absent loved ones. Bless the Church to which we belong. Give to our pastor wisdom and grace, and make him abundantly useful. Bless the sick, comfort the sorrowing, raise up the bowed down, and save all the people from their sins. Take care of us this night. Let our sleep be sweet and refreshing. May we arise in the morning full of gratitude, and with high purpose to do thy will. Sustain us through all our trials, and guide us through all our difficulties, and at last save us in heaven, for Christ's sake. Amen.

II. LESSON.   Psalm iv.

HEAR me when I call, O God of my righteousness: thou hast enlarged me when I was in distress; have mercy upon me, and hear my prayer. O ye sons of men, how long will ye turn my glory into shame? how long will ye love vanity, and seek after leasing? Selah. But know that the Lord hath set apart him that is godly for himself: the Lord will hear when I call unto him. Stand in awe, and sin not: commune with your own heart upon your bed, and be still. Selah. Offer the sacrifices of righteousness, and put your trust in the Lord. There be many that say, Who will show us any good? Lord, lift thou up the light of thy countenance upon us. Thou hast put gladness in my heart, more than in the time that their corn and their wine increased. I will both lay me down in peace and sleep; for thou, Lord, only makest me dwell in safety.

8, 7s.

SAVIOUR, breathe an evening blessing,
  Ere repose our spirits seal;
Sin and want we come confessing;
  Thou canst save and thou canst heal.

Though destruction walk around us,
  Though the arrow past us fly,
Angel guards from thee surround us;
  We are safe if thou art nigh.

Monday Evening.

PRAYER.

We thank thee, O God, for the strength and the will to work during the day; that thou hast given us our daily bread; that we are gathered under roof for the night; that no harm has come to us; that our fears have been disappointed; that we have been delivered from unreasonable men; and that thy providence and thy grace have been our help and our safety. We confess, our Father, that we have failed to be as true to ourselves, as just toward others, and as lovingly trustful of thee as we should have been; but hitherto thou hast helped us, and we would that thy loving-kindness should lead us to repentance and amendment. We pray thee to strengthen us in our convictions of right, of duty, and of love, and rid us of personal weakness, of suspicion of our fellows, and distrust of thee. Help us to make a better record to-morrow. May the shame of our short-comings and sins restrain us from further neglects and transgressions. May we begin the morrow with a larger capital of purpose and grace than ever, and may it be so put out to usury that greater good may come to us and greater glory to thy name. Bless the hearts and the homes of our community. Make each family a center of Christian influence; and as new homes are made, let new altars arise and thy worship continue to the last generation. That this Christian succession may go on, convert our sons and daughters, and early number them among thy spiritual children. And thine shall be the glory of our and their salvation through Christ the Lord. Amen.

III. LESSON. Psalm cxxi.

I WILL lift up mine eyes unto the hills, from whence cometh my help. My help cometh from the Lord, which made heaven and earth. He will not suffer thy foot to be moved; he that keepeth thee will not slumber. Behold, he that keepeth Israel shall neither slumber nor sleep. The Lord is thy keeper; the Lord is thy shade upon thy right-hand. The sun shall not smite thee by day, nor the moon by night. The Lord shall preserve thee from all evil; he shall preserve thy soul. The Lord shall preserve thy going out and thy coming in from this time forth, and even for evermore.

How much better is it to get wisdom than gold? and to get understanding rather to be chosen than silver? Pride goeth before destruction, and a haughty spirit before a fall.

Proverbs xvi. 16. 18

S. M.

Lord, in the strength of grace,
  With a glad heart and free,
Myself, my residue of days,
  I consecrate to thee.

Thy ransomed servant, I
  Restore to thee thy own;
And, from this moment, live or die,
  To serve my God alone.

PRAYER.

Most merciful and ever blessed God, thou art the fountain of life; in thee all good is treasured, and from thee all good proceeds. We come to thee for life, for strength, for wisdom, grace, and peace. We come before thee asking these blessings, and that each day they may be renewed to us. Thou hast said, "I am come that ye might have life, and have it more abundantly." O Lord of life, increase thy life in us, and make it abundant. Fill us with thyself, stimulate our growth, sustain our spiritual affections, refresh our zeal, and mold us to thy pure likeness. Endow us with the gift of life—life for worship, and life for work. Give us thy abiding peace, and may it rule in our hearts and harmonize all our feelings; may its presence and influence never be lessened in us. When temptations arise, may thy Spirit calm us by its sweet constraint, so that our energies shall move freely in thy service, and our hearts be ready for every duty. O Father, hear this prayer, and grant us, for Jesus' sake, its rich and ceaseless answer as long as life shall last. Amen.

IV. LESSON. Psalm cxix. 97-112.

O how love I thy law! it is my meditation all the day. Thou through thy commandments hast made me wiser than mine enemies; for they are ever with me. I have more understanding than all my teachers; for thy testimonies are my meditation. I understand more than the ancients, because I keep thy precepts. I have refrained my feet from every evil way, that I might keep thy word. I have not departed from thy judgments; for thou hast taught me. How sweet are thy words unto my taste! yea, sweeter than honey to my mouth. Through thy precepts I get understanding; therefore I hate every false way. Thy word is a lamp unto my feet, and a light unto my path. I have sworn, and I will perform it, that I will keep thy righteous judgments. I am afflicted very much; quicken me, O Lord, according unto thy word. Accept, I beseech thee, the free-will offerings of my mouth, O Lord, and teach me thy judgments. My soul is continually in my hand; yet do I not forget thy law. The wicked have laid a snare for me; yet I erred not from thy precepts. Thy testimonies have I taken as a heritage forever; for they are the rejoicing of my heart. I have inclined mine heart to perform thy statutes always, even unto the end.

7s.

Children of the Heavenly King,
As we journey, let us sing;
Sing our Saviour's worthy praise,
Glorious in his works and ways.

We are trav'ling home to God,
In the way our fathers trod;
They are happy now, and we
Soon their happiness shall see.

PRAYER.

O Lord, our Lord, how excellent is thy name in all the earth! who hath set thy glory above the heavens. When we consider thy heavens, the work of thy fingers, the moon and the stars, which thou hast ordained; what is man that thou art mindful of him? and the son of man that thou visitest him? So teach us to number our days that we may apply our hearts unto wisdom. Let thy work appear unto thy servants, and thy glory unto our children; and establish thou the work of our hands upon us; yea, the work of our hands, establish thou it. O Lord, righteousness belongeth unto thee, but unto us confusion of faces, because we have sinned against thee. We know that in us dwelleth no good thing; for to will is present with us; but how to perform that which is good, we find not. For, though we delight in thy law, after the inward man, we see another law in our members, warring against the law of our mind, and bringing us into captivity to the law of sin which is in our members. Purge us with hyssop, and we shall be clean; wash us, and we shall be whiter than snow. Hide thy face from our sins, and blot out all our iniquities. Create in us clean hearts, O God; and renew right spirits within us. Cast us not away from thy presence; and take not thy Holy Spirit from us. Restore unto us the joy of thy salvation; and uphold us with thy Spirit. So shall we teach transgressors thy free ways; and sinners shall be converted unto thee. We bless thy name, O Lord, that thou art merciful and gracious, slow to anger, and plenteous in mercy. Thou hast not dealt with us after our sins, nor rewarded us according to our iniquities. For, as the heaven is high above the earth, so great is thy mercy toward them that fear thee. For thou knowest our frame; thou rememberest that we are dust. As we assemble now around the family altar, we worship thee as our Father and our God. From thee alone have come to us the blessings we enjoy; and we desire to dedicate afresh to thee ourselves, with all we have and are. And though we be unworthy of thy notice, we beseech thee for thy Son our Saviour's sake accept and own us as thy children. Use us in thy vineyard as humble laborers, by whom thy cause may be extended and our fellow-men be blessed. May it be our constant aim to set before our neighbors examples worthy of their imitation, and by every possible means to show forth the principles of our holy religion. Look tenderly to-night, we pray thee, on all who suffer. As through the weary watches they long for the morning, may the light of thy countenance cheer and bless them, and enable them to trust thee, even though thou slay them. Be ever present with all who labor for the welfare of mankind. Bless every proper effort made to check intemperance and vice, and to establish peace and order among men. Cause wars to cease in the earth, that harmony and happiness may reign in all lands. And now, O Father, we commend ourselves to thy care for the night. Give us sweet sleep and quiet rest, that we may rise refreshed and ready for the duties of the morrow. Direct us through the remnant of our lives in all our goings; and afterward receive us to thyself on high, for Jesus' sake. Amen.

THE law of the Lord is perfect, converting the soul; the testimony of the Lord is sure, making wise the simple. The statutes of the Lord are right, rejoicing the heart; the commandment of the Lord is pure, enlightening the eyes. The fear of the Lord is clean, enduring forever; the judgments of the Lord are true and righteous altogether. More to be desired are they than gold, yea, than much fine gold; sweeter also than honey and the honeycomb. Moreover by them is thy servant warned; and in keeping of them there is great reward. Who can understand his errors? cleanse thou me from secret faults. Keep back thy servant also from presumptuous sins; let them not have dominion over me; then shall I be upright, and I shall be innocent from the great transgression. Let the words of my mouth, and the meditation of my heart, be acceptable in thy sight, O Lord, my strength, and my redeemer. Psalm xix. 7-14.

Services for Tuesday Morning.

I. LESSON. Luke xii. 22-37.

AND he said unto his disciples, Therefore I say unto you, Take no thought for your life, what ye shall eat; neither for the body, what ye shall put on. The life is more than meat, and the body is more than raiment. Consider the ravens: for they neither sow nor reap: which neither have store-house nor barn; and God feedeth them. How much more are ye better than the fowls? And which of you with taking thought can add to his stature one cubit? If ye then be not able to do that thing which is least, why take ye thought for the rest? Consider the lilies how they grow: they toil not, they spin not; and yet I say unto you, that Solomon in all his glory was not arrayed like one of these. If then God so clothe the grass, which is to-day in the field, and to-morrow is cast into the oven; how much more will he clothe you, O ye of little faith? And seek not ye what ye shall eat, or what ye shall drink, neither be ye of doubtful mind. For all these things do the nations of the world seek after; and your Father knoweth that ye have need of these things. But rather seek ye the kingdom of God, and all these things shall be added unto you. Fear not, little flock; for it is your Father's good pleasure to give you the kingdom. Sell that ye have, and give alms: provide yourselves bags which wax not old, a treasure in the heavens that faileth not, where no thief approacheth, neither moth corrupteth. For where your treasure is, there will your heart be also. Let your loins be girded about, and your lights burning; and ye yourselves like unto men that wait for their lord, when he will return from the wedding; that, when he cometh and knocketh, they may open unto him immediately. Blessed are those servants, whom the lord when he cometh shall find watching: verily I say unto you, that he shall gird himself, and make them to sit down to meat, and will come forth and serve them.

God is our refuge and strength, a very present help in trouble. *Psalm xlvi. 1.*

7s.

Day by day the manna fell:
O to learn this lesson well!
Still by constant mercy fed,
Give me, Lord, my daily bread.
"Day by day," the promise reads,
Daily strength for daily needs;
Cast foreboding fears away;
Take the manna of to-day.

PRAYER.

O God, our Heavenly Father, we thank thee for thy preserving care during the night, and for the use of our minds and bodies this morning. May we employ all our powers this day in accordance with thy holy will. We thank thee for thy word, and for thy Son, Jesus Christ, who died to redeem us from sin and death. For his sake, we pray thee, forgive us our sins, and guide us this day by thy good Spirit, that we may do justly, love mercy, and walk humbly with thee. Give us the witness of thy Spirit with ours that our sins are forgiven. Incline and strengthen us unto all good, and restrain us from all evil. Comfort us, we beseech thee, O our Father, in our sorrows, heal us of our afflictions, enlighten us in darkness, and guide and keep us in times of doubt and trial. Lord, we would commit into thy hands all we have and are. Sanctify our hearts, purify our thoughts, and make us altogether well-pleasing in thy sight. Bless our friends, our neighbors, and our enemies. May thy Church prosper, and thy kingdom prevail in all the earth. Give the consolations of thy grace unto all who call upon thee in any distress. Mightily aid every good cause, and thwart and overthrow every agency of evil.

Help us to do our duty in the furtherance of truth and righteousness in the earth, and save us at last, for Christ's sake. Amen.

II. LESSON. Proverbs iii. 5–18.

Trust in the Lord with all thine heart; and lean not unto thine own understanding. In all thy ways, acknowledge him, and he shall direct thy paths. Be not wise in thine own eyes; fear the Lord, and depart from evil. It shall be health to thy navel, and marrow to thy bones. Honor the Lord with thy substance, and with the first-fruits of all thine increase: so shall thy barns be filled with plenty, and thy presses shall burst out with new wine. My son, despise not the chastening of the Lord; neither be weary of his correction; for whom the Lord loveth he correcteth; even as a father the son in whom he delighteth. Happy is the man that findeth wisdom, and the man that getteth understanding; for the merchandise of it is better than the merchandise of silver, and the gain thereof than fine gold. She is more precious than rubies; and all the things thou canst desire are not to be compared unto her. Length of days is in her right-hand; and in her left-hand riches and honor. Her ways are ways of pleasantness, and all her paths are peace. She is a tree of life to them that lay hold upon her; and happy is every one that retaineth her.

S. M.

Commit thou all thy griefs
   And ways into His hands,
To His sure trust and tender care,
   Who earth and heaven commands:
Who points the clouds their course,
   Whom winds and seas obey,
He shall direct thy wand'ring feet,
   He shall prepare thy way.

PRAYER.

Help us, O our God, to feel in our hearts what we utter in our prayers. May we justly prize the precious privilege of worshiping thee. May it always be our chief delight to do thy will. As we remember thy amazing goodness and love, may we truly repent of all our sins against thee. Pardon all our unfaithfulness, and fill us with the peace and joy of the sons and daughters of God. As we enter upon the duties of this day, reveal unto us what it is thy will that we shall do. In all our thoughts and plans, in all our labors and pleasures, may we be guided by thy wisdom, supplied by thy providence, and kept humble and righteous by thy grace. Keep us mindful that thine eye is always upon us, and that thou knowest the very secrets of our souls. Lead us to compare all our thoughts and desires, and habits and examples, and labors and amusements, and hopes and fears, with thy plain and faithful word. Accept our fervent thanks for all thy mercies unto us, unto all we love, unto all mankind. Bless all who need thee, according to thy righteousness and love in Jesus Christ. Sanctify all our experience this day, and through all our future life, to the good of our souls, the happiness of our fellow-men, and the glory of thy name. We give our all to thee, and pray thy blessing for time and eternity through Jesus Christ, our Mediator and Redeemer. Amen.

WISDOM is better than rubies; and all the things that may be desired are not to be compared to it. The fear of the Lord is to hate evil; pride, and arrogancy, and the evil way, and the froward mouth do I hate. I love them that love me; and those that seek me early shall find me. Riches and honor are with me; yea, durable riches and righteousness. My fruit is better than gold, yea, than fine gold; and my revenue than choice silver.

Proverbs viii, 11, 13, 17-19.

III. LESSON.   Isaiah xxxv.

The wilderness and the solitary place shall be glad for them; and the desert shall rejoice, and blossom as the rose. It shall blossom abundantly, and rejoice even with joy and singing; the glory of Lebanon shall be given unto it, the excellency of Carmel and Sharon; they shall see the glory of the Lord, and the excellency of our God. Strengthen ye the weak hands, and confirm the feeble knees. Say to them that are of a fearful heart, Be strong, fear not; behold, your God will come with vengeance, even God with a recompense; he will come and save you. Then the eyes of the blind shall be opened, and the ears of the deaf shall be unstopped. Then shall the lame man leap as a hart, and the tongue of the dumb sing; for in the wilderness shall waters break out, and streams in the desert. And the parched ground shall become a pool, and the thirsty land springs of water; in the habitation of dragons, where each lay, shall be grass with reeds and rushes. And a highway shall be there, and a way, and it shall be called the way of holiness; the unclean shall not pass over it; but it shall be for those; the wayfaring men, though fools, shall not err therein. No lion shall be there, nor any ravenous beast shall go up thereon, it shall not be found there; but the redeemed shall walk there; and the ransomed of the Lord shall return, and come to Zion with songs and everlasting joy upon their heads; they shall obtain joy and gladness, and sorrow and sighing shall flee away.

O COME, let us sing unto the Lord; let us make a joyful noise to the Rock of our salvation. Let us come before his presence with thanksgiving, and make a joyful noise unto him with psalms. For the Lord is a great God, and a great King above all gods. In his hand are the deep places of the earth; the strength of the hills is his also. The sea is his, and he made it; and his hands formed the dry land. O come, let us worship and bow down; let us kneel before the Lord our maker. For he is our God; and we are the people of his pasture, and the sheep of his hand.   Psalm xcv. 1-7.

C. M.

JESUS, united by thy grace,
  And each to each endeared,
With confidence we seek thy face,
  And know our prayer is heard.
Still let us own our common Lord,
  And bear thine easy yoke;
A band of love, a threefold cord,
  Which never can be broke.

PRAYER.

We thank thee, O Lord, for the beautiful and instructive and comforting lesson which has just been read out of the Holy Book. Thou art our Father, and we approach thee as thy needy children, most humbly praying that thou wouldst now verify the precious promises contained in thy Book. Help us to cast our burdens on thee, with the assurance that thou wilt sustain us. Guide us into all truth, strengthen us with might in the inner man. Help us to embrace in all its fullness the love of God.. Lead us by the still waters of thy grace. Impart to us the mind of the blessed Master. Fill us with all the fullness of God. Bless our family. May we live together according to thy holy ordinances, obeying thy commandments, and glorifying thy holy name. Succor us when we are tempted, and give us power to overcome every assault of the enemy. Save us from pride and vanity, from impatience, envy, and jealousy, from fretfulness, anger, wrath, and malice, and from all unholy associations and evil influences. Deliver us, O Lord, from every habit that tends to enslave us, and from every spirit which can involve us in sin or lead us away from thee. Thus may the day pass in the love and fear of God. These blessings we ask in the name of Jesus Christ our Lord. Amen.

IV. LESSON. 2 Peter i. 1-11.

SIMON PETER, a servant and an apostle of Jesus Christ, to them that have obtained like precious faith with us through the righteousness of God and our Saviour Jesus Christ: Grace and peace be multiplied unto you through the knowledge of God, and of Jesus our Lord, according as his divine power hath given unto us all things that pertain unto life and godliness, through the knowledge of him that hath called us to glory and virtue; whereby are given unto us exceeding great and precious promises; that by these ye might be partakers of the divine nature, having escaped the corruption that is in the world through lust. And besides this, giving all diligence, add to your faith virtue; and to virtue, knowledge; and to knowledge, temperance; and to temperance, patience; and to patience, godliness; and to godliness, brotherly kindness; and to brotherly kindness, charity. For if these things be in you, and abound, they make you that ye shall neither be barren nor unfruitful in the knowledge of our Lord Jesus Christ. But he that lacketh these things is blind, and cannot see afar off, and hath forgotten that he was purged from his old sins. Wherefore the rather, brethren, give diligence to make your calling and election sure; for if ye do these things, ye shall never fall; for so an entrance shall be ministered unto you abundantly into the everlasting kingdom of our Lord and Saviour Jesus Christ.

C. M.

My Saviour, my almighty Friend,
  When I begin thy praise,
Where will the growing numbers end,
  The numbers of thy grace?

Thou art my everlasting trust;
  Thy goodness I adore:
Send down thy grace, O blessed Lord,
  That I may love thee more.

PRAYER.

Once more we come before thee, our Father and our God, to praise thy name for all thy loving-kindnesses continued to us still. We have risen from our beds, refreshed by quiet sleep, and are ready to begin the labors of another day. Thou still suppliest us with food and every thing we need for life and duty. Thou blessest us with mutual sympathy and love, by which we enjoy each other's presence, and delight to labor for our common good. We worship thee as the Author of concord and the Prince of Peace; and we pray thee to implant in us more and more the peaceful principles of the gospel, that we may love thee supremely, and love our neighbors as ourselves. May we also love our enemies, bless them that curse us, do good to them that hate us, and pray for them which despitefully use us and persecute us, that we may be thy children in deed and in truth. As now we enter on the duties of the day, we would deeply feel our constant need of thy blessing and help in all our efforts. We would do nothing inconsistent with thy will, nothing on which thy blessing may not rest. Wean us, we pray thee, from every improper object of affection. Turn us away from every unworthy undertaking. Save us also from undue attachment even to the proper things of earth, which might divert our highest love from thee. May we use this world as not abusing it. May we remember that it is not our home. May we expect not here our highest joy, but look away to thee and heaven for perfect bliss. Yet grant us, Heavenly Father, God of love, O grant us every day some foretaste of the heavenly joy, as in the beamings of thy smiling face, and with good evidence of thine approval, we go about our daily work, trusting in thee. And grant to us this day such measure of success as may seem best to thee, withholding from us even what we most desire, if it would be injurious to us or to thy cause. But, whatsoever else thou givest or deniest, give us grace to yield to thee without a murmur, and to feel that all things work together for our good. We invoke thy blessings upon all classes of men: upon the rich, that they may be poor in spirit, trusting not in earthly good, but using their wealth for the promotion of thy glory; upon the poor, that they may be rich in faith, and may lay up their treasure in heaven; upon the sick, that they may intrust themselves to thee, as the Divine Physician, able to heal both body and soul; upon the bereaved, that they may find thee more than a substitute for their loved and lost ones; upon all in authority in Church and State, that they may rule in righteousness and in thy fear; upon the penitent, that they may be directed to the exercise of saving faith in Jesus Christ, thy Son, our Lord; upon the ungodly, that they may cease to do evil, and learn to do well; and upon thy people of every name, that they may live together in holy harmony, showing forth thy praise, and inducing others to devote themselves to thee. These things, O Father, and whatever else we need for this life or for the life to come, we humbly ask in the name and for the sake of Jesus Christ, our Lord, to whom, with thee and the Holy Ghost, be all praise and glory, both now and forever. Amen.

And he gave some, apostles; and some, prophets; and some, evangelists; and some, pastors and teachers; for the perfecting of the saints, for the work of the ministry, for the edifying of the body of Christ; till we all come in the unity of the faith, and of the knowledge of the Son of God, unto a perfect man, unto the measure of the stature of the fullness of Christ; that we henceforth be no more children, tossed to and fro, and carried about with every wind of doctrine, by the sleight of men, and cunning craftiness, whereby they lie in wait to deceive; but speaking the truth in love, may grow up into him in all things, which is the head, even Christ; from whom the whole body fitly joined together and compacted by that which every joint supplieth, according to the effectual working in the measure of every part, maketh increase of the body unto the edifying of itself in love. Ephesians iv. 11-16.

Services for Tuesday Evening.

I. LESSON. Matthew vi. 19-34.

LAY not up for yourselves treasures upon earth, where moth and rust doth corrupt, and where thieves break through and steal; but lay up for yourselves treasures in heaven, where neither moth nor rust doth corrupt, and where thieves do not break through nor steal; for where your treasure is, there will your heart be also. The light of the body is the eye; if therefore thine eye be single, thy whole body shall be full of light. But if thine eye be evil, thy whole body shall be full of darkness. If therefore the light that is in thee be darkness, how great is that darkness! No man can serve two masters; for either he will hate the one, and love the other; or else he will hold to the one, and despise the other. Ye cannot serve God and mammon. Therefore I say unto you, Take no thought for your life, what ye shall eat, or what ye shall drink; nor yet for your body, what ye shall put on. Is not the life more than meat, and the body more than raiment? Behold the fowls of the air; for they sow not, neither do they reap, nor gather into barns; yet your Heavenly Father feedeth them. Are ye not much better than they? Which of you by taking thought can add one cubit unto his stature? And why take ye thought for raiment? Consider the lilies of the field, how they grow; they toil not, neither do they spin; and yet I say unto you, That even Solomon in all his glory was not arrayed like one of these. Wherefore, if God so clothe the grass of the field, which to-day is, and to-morrow is cast into the oven, shall he not much more clothe you, O ye of little faith? Therefore take no thought, saying, What shall we eat? or, What shall we drink? or, Wherewithal shall we be clothed? (for after all these things do the Gentiles seek) for your Heavenly Father knoweth that ye have need of all these things. But seek ye first the kingdom of God, and his righteousness, and all these things shall be added unto you. Take therefore no thought for the morrow; for the morrow shall take thought for the things of itself. Sufficient unto the day is the evil thereof.

S. M.

The day is past and gone,
   The evening shades appear:
O may we all remember well,
   The night of death draws near!

Lord, keep us safe this night,
   Secure from all our fears;
May angels guard us, while we sleep,
   Till morning light appears.

PRAYER.

O LORD our God, thou makest the outgoings of the morning and the evening to rejoice. Thy merciful kindness has been over us during another day. We have had health and strength for the prosecution of our respective callings in life; and we gather to-night around the family altar to commemorate thy loving-kindness and to call upon thy name. We praise thee for all thy kind remembrance of us in the past; and constrained by thy mercies, would present our souls and bodies unto thee as a living sacrifice, which is our reasonable service. Forgive us if during this day we have been guilty of any impurity of thought, affection, or desire, any hastiness of temper, any improper word or act. Assure us, ere we retire to rest, that we have peace with God through our Lord Jesus Christ. As our days swiftly succeed one another, may we be reminded how brief and uncertain is our stay upon the earth, how soon our days will all be numbered. And as here we have no abiding-place, no continuing city, may we seek one to come—a city which hath foundations, whose maker and builder is God. May we lay up our treasures in heaven, and set our affections upon things above, and labor not for the meat that perisheth but for that which endureth unto eternal life. Have us under thy guardian care through this night season. Thou Shepherd of Israel, who neither slumberest nor sleepest, through the shades and slumbers of this night let thine ever-wakeful eye be upon us, and thy protecting arm round about us. May no evil befall us, nor any plague come nigh our dwelling. Bring us in health and safety to another day, and may we rise on the morrow prepared to consecrate ourselves anew to thy service. When the day of life shall close, as this day is about to close, and the shades of death's dark night gather around us, give us thy sustaining grace in that eventful hour. May we fall sweetly asleep in Jesus, and in the morning of the resurrection awake in his likeness, to the vision of his glory and the fruition of his presence forever. Amen.

I LOVE the Lord, because he hath heard my voice and my supplications. Because he hath inclined his ear unto me, therefore will I call upon him as long as I live. What shall I render unto the Lord for all his benefits toward me? I will take the cup of salvation, and call upon the name of the Lord.

Psalm cxvi. 1, 2, 12, 13

II. LESSON. Deut. vi. 1-9, 20-25.

Now these are the commandments, the statutes, and the judgments, which the Lord your God commanded to teach you, that ye might do them in the land whither ye go to possess it: That thou mightest fear the Lord thy God, to keep all his statutes and his commandments, which I command thee, thou, and thy son, and thy son's son, all the days of thy life; and that thy days may be prolonged. Hear therefore, O Israel, and observe to do it; that it may be well with thee, and that ye may increase mightily, as the Lord God of thy fathers hath promised thee, in the land that floweth with milk and honey. Hear, O Israel: The Lord our God is one Lord; and thou shalt love the Lord thy God with all thine heart, and with all thy soul, and with all thy might. And these words, which I command thee this day, shall be in thine heart; and thou shalt teach them diligently unto thy children, and shalt talk of them when thou sittest in thine house, and when thou walkest by the way, and when thou liest down, and when thou risest up. And thou shalt bind them for a sign upon thine hand, and they shall be as frontlets between thine eyes. And thou shalt write them upon the posts of thy house, and on thy gates. And when thy son asketh thee in time to come, saying, What mean the testimonies, and the statutes, and the judgments, which the Lord our God hath commanded you? then thou shalt say unto thy son, We were Pharaoh's bondmen in Egypt; and the Lord brought us out of Egypt with a mighty hand; and the Lord shewed signs and wonders, great and sore, upon Egypt, upon Pharaoh, and upon all his household, before our eyes; and he brought us out from thence, that he might bring us in, to give us the land which he sware unto our fathers. And the Lord commanded us to do all these statutes, to fear the Lord our God, for our good always, that he might preserve us alive, as it is at this day. And it shall be our righteousness, if we observe to do all these commandments before the Lord our God, as he hath commanded us.

C. M.

Through many dangers, toils, and snares,
  I have already come;
'T is grace has brought me safe thus far,
  And grace will lead me home.

The Lord has promised good to me—
  His word my hope secures:
He will my shield and portion be
  As long as life endures.

PRAYER.

O Lord, our gracious Heavenly Father, we bow in thy solemn presence at the close of this another day of our short life, in token of our dependence upon thee and submission to thy blessed will. We acknowledge thy manifold blessings and tender mercies in all past life, and especially during the day just now closing. But in considering thy goodness to us in the past, we would not forget that thou art present with us now. At this very moment thou, God, seest us. O may a sense of thy presence inspire our devotions and spiritualize our worship. And in view of thy great goodness to us, and our unfaithfulness to thee, may we be humbled in dust at thy feet; and realizing our utter helplessness and entire dependence, may we be enabled to rely upon the merits of our blessed Saviour, in whose name only we come. O grant that through him we may receive forgiveness of all that is past, and realize in our own consciousness that we are at peace with thee. With us, bless all the subjects of our prayers, especially all that have asked us to pray for them, or that desire an interest in our devotions. Bind up the hearts that sorrow has broken; be tender to the aged and feeble, the sick and dying, and all that are in any way distressed; and may all remember with joy that "earth has no sorrows that heaven cannot heal." Bless our friends, and have mercy upon our enemies (if we have them). And now, Lord, we commit us unto thee—all that we have and are. Be very near us to-night, guide us through life, make us useful in the world, comfort us with thy presence in death, and in heaven save us all, with all for whom we may pray, we humbly ask for the great Redeemer's sake. Amen.

III. LESSON. Psalm xxv. 1-14.

UNTO thee, O Lord, do I lift up my soul. O my God, I trust in thee; let me not be ashamed, let not mine enemies triumph over me. Yea, let none that wait on thee be ashamed; let them be ashamed which transgress without cause. Shew me thy ways, O Lord; teach me thy paths. Lead me in thy truth, and teach me; for thou art the God of my salvation; on thee do I wait all the day. Remember, O Lord, thy tender mercies and thy loving-kindnesses; for they have been ever of old. Remember not the sins of my youth, nor my transgressions; according to thy mercy remember thou me for thy goodness' sake, O Lord. Good and upright is the Lord; therefore will he teach sinners in the way. The meek will he guide in judgment; and the meek will he teach his way. All the paths of the Lord are mercy and truth unto such as keep his covenant and his testimonies. For thy name's sake, O Lord, pardon mine iniquity; for it is great. What man is he that feareth the Lord? him shall he teach in the way that he shall choose. His soul shall dwell at ease; and his seed shall inherit the earth. The secret of the Lord is with them that fear him; and he will shew them his covenant.

C. M.

Once more we come before our God;
  Once more his blessings ask:
O may not duty seem a load,
  Nor worship prove a task!

Father, thy quick'ning Spirit send
  From heaven in Jesus' name,
To make our waiting minds attend,
  And put our souls in frame.

PRAYER.

Most merciful and ever blessed God, every day's experience proves that we can only be happy with thy love in our hearts. The nearer we get to thee the stronger we are. O then, merciful Father, let nothing come between thee and us. Cleanse our hearts daily, give us power over all sin, hallow our minds, sweeten our spirits, make us Christ-like, and supply in us all that is needed to effect entire conformity to all thy righteous will. Let no mental taste rise into rivalry with thy authority, but sanctify all tastes and all thoughts, and may thy glory be the end of all our works and the guardian angel of all our pleasures. Fill our souls with thy love, and strengthen our yearnings after purity. Thou knowest what we need to qualify us for the demands and duties of life. Ceaselessly shine on our minds and hearts, strengthen and sustain our bodily health, and quicken our spiritual natures faithfully to serve thee. Grant us repose and restful sleep during the darkness, and may no evil come nigh our dwelling. May all our interests be precious in thy sight. Bless our loved ones and kindred, and bring our common humanity throughout the wide world to thee. We offer these prayers through thee, our blessed Saviour and Mediator. Amen.

IV. LESSON. Prov. i. 7, 10, 24-31.

THE fear of the Lord is the beginning of knowledge; but fools despise wisdom and instruction. My son, if sinners entice thee, consent thou not. Because I have called, and ye refused; I have stretched out my hand, and no man regarded; but ye have set at naught all my counsel, and would none of my reproof; I also will laugh at your calamity; I will mock when your fear cometh; when your fear cometh as desolation, and your destruction cometh as a whirlwind; when distress and anguish cometh upon you. Then shall they call upon me, but I will not answer; they shall seek me early, but they shall not find me; for that they hated knowledge, and did not choose the fear of the Lord; they would none of my counsel; they despised all my reproof. Therefore shall they eat of the fruit of their own way, and be filled with their own devices.

L. M.

My God, how endless is thy love!
    Thy gifts are every evening new;
And morning mercies from above
    Gently distill like early dew.

I yield myself to thy command;
    To thee devote my nights and days:
Perpetual blessings from thy hand
    Demand perpetual songs of praise.

PRAYER.

At the close of another day, O Lord, we come together before thee, desiring to present ourselves and our prayers and praises in the name of our Saviour Jesus Christ, praising thee most of all that we have access to thee through him. We bless thee for the perfect atonement made for our sins by his sufferings and death; that he was wounded for our transgressions, he was bruised for our iniquities, he was delivered for our offenses, and was raised again for our justification. Truly thou commendest thy love toward us, in that, while we were yet sinners, Christ died for us. We praise thy name also that through him thou hast given us all the blessings of thy providence that have fallen to our happy lot. Throughout the day now closing we have had food and clothing, health and reason, strength to labor, and useful work to do. Thou hast given us neither poverty nor riches, but enough of the good things of this life to secure our comfort without destroying our sense of dependence upon thee. Help us to commit ourselves to thy fatherly care for the night which is upon us, and to feel sure that thou wilt ward off from our dwelling every evil thing. Give us refreshing rest and quiet sleep, and power to rise in the morning prepared for all the cares and duties of the day. And so, from day to day, go with us all along the journey of our lives, causing thy face to shine upon us, and ever granting us thy peace. Besides ourselves, we would intrust to thee our absent friends and kindred. Thou knowest their several wants; thou knowest how great a debt of gratitude we owe them for their kindness to us, and how our hearts go out in earnest longing for their welfare. Repay them, Heavenly Father, as we cannot, for all their kindly services to us; and pour thy blessings on them as they need, both for this life and for the life to come. Be very gracious, merciful Father, to all who suffer, whether in mind, in body, or in estate. May they have grace to feel that their affliction is but for a moment, and worketh for them a far more exceeding and eternal weight of glory. And grant them such relief from their distresses as shall be really best for them, and most conducive through them to the glory of thy name. Look with favor on all proper efforts which are made for the improvement of the rising race. Bless all teachers in our colleges and schools, and those engaged in Sunday-school work. May they succeed in training the young for stations of useful labor here below, and for endless bliss on high. And now unto Him that loved us, and washed us from our sins in his own blood, to him be glory and dominion forever and ever. Amen.

Services for Wednesday Morning.

I. LESSON. Luke xii. 32-40.

FEAR not, little flock; for it is your Father's good pleasure to give you the kingdom. Sell that ye have, and give alms; provide yourselves bags which wax not old, a treasure in the heavens that faileth not, where no thief approacheth, neither moth corrupteth. For where your treasure is, there will your heart be also. Let your loins be girded about, and your lights burning; and ye yourselves like unto men that wait for their lord, when he will return from the wedding; that, when he cometh and knocketh, they may open unto him immediately. Blessed are those servants, whom the lord when he cometh shall find watching; verily I say unto you, that he shall gird himself, and make them to sit down to meat, and will come forth and serve them. And if he shall come in the second watch, or come in the third watch, and find them so, blessed are those servants. And this know, that if the good man of the house had known what hour the thief would come, he would have watched, and not have suffered his house to be broken through. Be ye therefore ready also; for the Son of man cometh at an hour when ye think not.

S. M.

Jesus, my truth, my way,
  My sure, unerring light,
On thee my feeble steps I stay,
  Which thou wilt guide aright.

My wisdom and my guide,
  My counselor thou art;
O never let me leave thy side,
  Or from thy paths depart.

PRAYER.

Our Heavenly Father, help us, as we come to thee, to trust only in the blood of Jesus. In thy great mercy prepare us to worship thee. May we feel our unworthiness and our utter dependence upon thee. Show us our sins in their true character, and enable us humbly and sorrowfully to confess them unto thee. Pardon us for all forgetfulness of thy will, for all indifference toward thy blessed cause, for all unrighteous love of the things of this world, for all our ingratitude to thee, for all our abuses of the gifts of thy kind providence, and for any other violation of our duty to thee. Give us now the testimony that thy loving favor is resting upon us. We thank thee that thou hast prolonged our lives; and that, with so many precious mercies, thou hast given us so much power to enjoy and improve them. We bless thee for all that has given us strength and comfort and hope and joy. We thank thee for the assurance that thy grace shall be sufficient for us, and that, if we be faithful, all shall work together for good to us. To thee we commit all our interests for this life and for the life to come. O guide us so that we may safely pass the dangers and temptations that may beset us, and may willingly perform all the duties thou mayest require of us, until it is thy good pleasure to receive us into thy "house not made with hands, eternal in the heavens;" where at last we may meet, to dwell together in endless happiness, and to praise thee for evermore. Amen.

II. LESSON. Psalm lxxxiv.

How amiable are thy tabernacles, O Lord of hosts! My soul longeth, yea, even fainteth for the courts of the Lord; my heart and my flesh crieth out for the living God. Yea, the sparrow hath found a house, and the swallow a nest for herself, where she may lay her young, even thine altars, O Lord of hosts, my King, and my God. Blessed are they that dwell in thy house; they will be still praising thee. Selah. Blessed is the man whose strength is in thee; in whose heart are the ways of them. Who passing through the valley of Baca make it a well; the rain also filleth the pools. They go from strength to strength, every one of them in Zion appeareth before God. O Lord God of hosts, hear my prayer; give ear, O God of Jacob. Selah. Behold, O God our shield, and look upon the face of thine anointed. For a day in thy courts is better than a thousand. I had rather be a door-keeper in the house of my God, than to dwell in the tents of wickedness. For the Lord God is a sun and shield; the Lord will give grace and glory; no good thing will he withhold from them that walk uprightly. O Lord of hosts, blessed is the man that trusteth in thee.

L. M.

God of my life whose gracious power
   Through various deaths my soul hath led,
Or turned aside the fatal hour,
   Or lifted up my sinking head!

In all my ways thy hand I own,
   Thy ruling providence I see;
Assist me still my course to run,
   And still direct my paths to thee.

PRAYER.

We thank thee, O Lord, for the coming of the morning, and all the mercies it brings us.

We feel our weakness and dependence upon thee, and now we come seeking grace for this day's duties and trials. Forgive our sins, and grant us grace to run with patience the race that is set before us, that we may glorify thee in our bodies and spirits, which are thine. May we have no other gods before thee, but may we love thee with our whole heart, soul, mind, and strength, and our neighbor as ourselves. Be thou our arm every morning, our salvation also in the time of trouble. May each of us go forth to duty conscious of thy presence, and may we be able to pass this day in the love and fear and service of our God, in the comfort of the Holy Spirit, and in imitation of thy Son our Saviour. Extend thy light and thy salvation to all the homes of our land and to all lands, till the world shall come to the saving knowledge of the one and only true God, and of his Son Jesus Christ; and thy name shall have the praise evermore. Amen.

III. LESSON.   Luke vi. 27-36.

BUT I say unto you which hear, Love your enemies, do good to them which hate you, bless them that curse you, and pray for them which despitefully use you. And unto him that smiteth thee on the one cheek offer also the other; and him that taketh away thy cloak forbid not to take thy coat also. Give to every man that asketh of thee; and of him that taketh away thy goods ask them not again. And as ye would that men should do to you, do ye also to them likewise. For if ye love them which love you, what thank have ye? for sinners also love those that love them. And if ye do good to them which do good to you, what thank have ye? for sinners also do even the same. And if ye lend to them of whom ye hope to receive, what thank have ye? for sinners also lend to sinners, to receive as much again. But love ye your enemies, and do good, and lend, hoping for nothing again; and your reward shall be great, and ye shall be the children of the Highest; for he is kind unto the unthankful and to the evil. Be ye therefore merciful, as your Father also is merciful.

C. M.

Giver and guardian of my sleep,
   To praise thy name I wake:
Still, Lord, thy helpless servant keep,
   For thine own mercy's sake.

The blessing of another day
   I thankfully receive:
O may I only thee obey,
   And to thy glory live.

PRAYER.

O Lord, our Heavenly Father, as we begin thy worship, may we draw nigh to thee, that thou mayest draw nigh to us. Teach us to understand those words of Jesus, "No man cometh unto the Father but by me." May our faith be consistent with thy promises, thy power, and thy love. In Jesus' name we pray thee to prepare us for this day. Cleanse us from all sin, receive our loving praises for all thy mercy, and kindle within us sincere desires for communion with thee. Save us from cold formality in using the means of grace. May we read thy word to learn thy will. Let our prayers and songs be full of fervor, faith, and love. Inspire and guide our thoughts and feelings, and enable us to receive with thankfulness and improve with devotion all the lessons thou wouldst teach us. May we to-day enjoy sweet peace in thee, and be permitted at last, as one by one we pass from earth, to enter and enjoy together the rest that remaineth for the people of God. Bless our kindred and loved ones, and let thy good providence and grace reach and save all mankind; and thine shall be the glory forever, through Jesus Christ our Redeemer. Amen.

IV. LESSON.   Psalm xci.

He that dwelleth in the secret place of the Most High shall abide under the shadow of the Almighty. I will say of the Lord, He is my refuge and my fortress; my God; in him will I trust. Surely he shall deliver thee from the snare of the fowler, and from the noisome pestilence. He shall cover thee with his feathers, and under his wings shalt thou trust; his truth shall be thy shield and buckler. Thou shalt not be afraid for the terror by night; nor for the arrow that flieth by day; nor for the pestilence that walketh in darkness; nor for the destruction that wasteth at noonday. A thousand shall fall at thy side, and ten thousand at thy right-hand; but it shall not come nigh thee. Only with thine eyes shalt thou behold and see the reward of the wicked. Because thou hast made the Lord, which is my refuge, even the Most High, thy habitation; there shall no evil befall thee, neither shall any plague come nigh thy dwelling. For he shall give his angels charge over thee, to keep thee in all thy ways. They shall bear thee up in their hands, lest thou dash thy foot against a stone. Thou shalt tread upon the lion and adder; the young lion and the dragon shalt thou trample under feet. Because he hath set his love upon me, therefore will I deliver him; I will set him on high, because he hath known my name. He shall call upon me, and I will answer him; I will be with him in trouble; I will deliver him, and honor him. With long life will I satisfy him, and shew him my salvation.

Give us help from trouble; for vain is the help of man. Psalm cviii. 12.

S. M.

See how the morning sun
  Pursues his shining way,
And wide proclaims his Maker's praise,
  With every bright'ning ray.

Thus would my rising soul
  Its heavenly Parent sing;
And to its great Original
  The humble tribute bring.

PRAYER.

O Lord, thou hast searched us and known us. Thou compassest our path and our lying down, and art acquainted with all our ways. For there is not a word in our tongue, but lo, O Lord, thou knowest it altogether. Whither shall we go from thy Spirit? or whither shall we flee from thy presence? If we ascend up into heaven, thou art there; if we make our bed in hell, behold, thou art there; if we take the wings of the morning, and dwell in the uttermost parts of the sea, even there shall thy hand lead us, and thy right-hand shall hold us. If we say, "Surely the darkness shall cover us," even the night shall be light about us. Yea, the darkness hideth not from thee; but the night shineth as the day; the darkness and the light are both alike to thee. How precious also are thy thoughts unto us, O God; how great is the sum of them. If we should count them, they are more in number than the sand; when we awake, we are still with thee. Search us, O God, and know our hearts; try us, and know our thoughts; and see if there be any wicked way in us, and lead us in the way everlasting. And now, as thou hast spared us through the shades of night, be with us also in our waking hours, and bless us as thou seest best throughout the day. If thou wilt help us, we cannot fail in any thing we undertake; and we can do nothing good without thy smile. Turn our hearts away from every thing that is wrong, and give us earnest interest in every good word and work. Whatsoever our hands find to do, may we do it with our might. May we exercise ourselves to have always consciences void of offense toward thee and toward men. We pray thee to make each one of us this day in some way useful to our fellow-men. May we bear one another's burdens, and so fulfill the law of Christ. May we imitate our Saviour's example, as he went about doing good. Let all bitterness and wrath and anger and clamor and evil-speaking be put away from us, with all malice; and may we be kind to one another, tender-hearted, forgiving one another, as thou for Christ's sake hast forgiven us. Heavenly Father, bless with us all thine earthly creatures. Thou knowest their hearts, their circumstances, their needs. O suit thy blessings to their cases, according to thy perfect knowledge of their wants, and according to thy tender compassion toward them. Pour thy Spirit richly upon all thy children, that they may show forth thy praise in their daily lives, and may induce many of their ungodly fellows to embrace the truth as it is in Jesus. O let the wickedness of the wicked come to an end, but establish the just; for thou, the righteous God, triest the hearts and reins. And now, O Lord, hear thou our prayer and our supplication in heaven, thy dwelling-place, and maintain our cause, and forgive our sins, and bless us, and save us, for Jesus' sake. Amen.

Services for Wednesday Evening.

I. LESSON. Matt. vi. 5-15, 24-33.

AND when thou prayest, thou shalt not be as the hypocrites are; for they love to pray standing in the synagogues and in the corners of the streets, that they may be seen of men. Verily I say unto you, They have their reward. But thou, when thou prayest, enter into thy closet, and when thou hast shut thy door, pray to thy Father which is in secret; and thy Father which seeth in secret shall reward thee openly. But when ye pray, use not vain repetitions, as the heathen do; for they think that they shall be heard for their much speaking. Be not ye therefore like unto them; for your Father knoweth what things ye have need of, before ye ask him. After this manner therefore pray ye: Our Father which art in heaven, hallowed be thy name. Thy kingdom come. Thy will be done in earth, as it is heaven. Give us this day our daily bread. And forgive us our debts, as we forgive our debtors. And lead us not into temptation, but deliver us from evil; for thine is the kingdom, and the power, and the glory, forever. Amen. For if ye forgive men their trespasses, your Heavenly Father will also forgive you; but if ye forgive not men their trespasses, neither will your Father forgive your trespasses. No man can serve two masters; for either he will hate the one, and love the other; or else he will hold to the one, and despise the other. Ye cannot serve God and mammon. Therefore I say unto you, Take no thought for your life, what ye shall eat, or what ye shall drink; nor yet for your body, what ye shall put on. Is not the life more than meat, and the body than raiment? Behold the fowls of the air; for they sow not, neither do they reap, nor gather into barns; yet your Heavenly Father feedeth them. Are ye not much better than they? Which of you by taking thought can add one cubit unto his stature? And why take ye thought for raiment? Consider the lilies of the field, how they grow; they toil not, neither do they spin; and yet I say unto you, That even Solomon in all his glory was not arrayed like one of these. Wherefore, if God so clothe the grass of the field, which to-day is, and to-morrow is cast into the oven, shall he not much more clothe you, O ye of little faith? Therefore take no thought, saying, What shall we eat? or, What shall we drink? or, Wherewithal shall we be clothed? (for after all these things do the Gentiles seek); for your Heavenly Father knoweth that ye have need of all these things. But seek ye first the kingdom of God, and his righteousness; and all these things shall be added unto you.

L. M.

ALL praise to thee, my God, this night,
For all the blessings of the light:
Keep me, O keep me, King of kings,
Under thine own almighty wings.

Forgive me, Lord, for thy dear Son,
The ills that I this day have done ;
That with the world, myself, and thee,
I, ere I sleep, at peace may be.

PRAYER.

How rich are thy mercies, O Lord, our strength and our Redeemer. Our hearts would praise thee for thy goodness; our lips would sing forth thy praises. Thou crownest every day with thy goodness. Accept, we beseech thee, in the name of thy Son Jesus Christ, our tribute of gratitude and praise for thy love and blessing during this day. Pardon whatsoever thou hast beheld amiss in our words, thoughts, and acts, and sanctify by thy Spirit this day's labor to thy glory and our spiritual good. May we evermore render to thee and thee alone the homage of our hearts. May our souls delight to bow down to thee and serve thee, and may our lives show forth in rich fruitage thy love shed abroad in our hearts. May we grow day by day in grace and in the knowledge of our Lord Jesus Christ, till we all come in the unity of the faith, and of the knowledge of the Son of God, unto perfect men, unto the measure of the stature of the fullness of Christ. May we retire to-night with consciences void of offense toward God and men. Let thy healing presence be felt at this hour by the hearts over which shades of sorrow have settled, and to whom this may be a night of pain and weariness of spirit. Give to them beauty for ashes, the oil of joy for mourning, and the garment of praise for the spirit of heaviness. Hear us, we beseech thee, in the name of thy Son and our Saviour Jesus Christ, to whom be glory forever. Amen.

II. LESSON. Psalm ciii. 1-18.

BLESS the Lord, O my soul; and all that is within me, bless his holy name. Bless the Lord, O my soul, and forget not all his benefits; who forgiveth all thine iniquities; who healeth all thy diseases; who redeemeth thy life from destruction; who crowneth thee with loving-kindness and tender mercies; who satisfieth thy mouth with good things; so that thy youth is renewed like the eagle's. The Lord executeth righteousness and judgment for all that are oppressed. He made known his ways unto Moses, his acts unto the children of Israel. The Lord is merciful and gracious, slow to anger, and plenteous in mercy. He will not always chide; neither will he keep his anger forever. He hath not dealt with us after our sins; nor rewarded us according to our iniquities. For as the heaven is high above the earth, so great is his mercy toward them that fear him. As far as the east is from the west, so far hath he removed our transgressions from us. Like as a father pitieth his children, so the Lord pitieth them that fear him. For he knoweth our frame; he remembereth that we are dust. As for man, his days are as grass; as a flower of the field, so he flourisheth. For the wind passeth over it, and it is gone; and the place thereof shall know it no more. But the mercy of the Lord is from everlasting to everlasting upon them that fear him, and his righteousness unto children's children; to such as keep his covenant, and to those that remember his commandments to do them.

8, 7.
Should swift death this night o'ertake us,
  And our couch become our tomb,
May the morn in heaven awake us,
  Clad in light, and deathless bloom.

PRAYER.

We thank thee, O Lord, that thou hast revealed thyself as our keeper. Since thou art for us, we have no fear of enemies, for thou art omnipotent. Our bodies need repose, but he who keepeth us needeth not to slumber. Thy faithfulness in the past is our hope for the future; therefore will we lay us to sleep in peace. Forgive our sins, and let them not be remembered in judgment against us. Wash our hearts from all stains of guilt so that they may be clean in thy sight. May thy love dwell in our hearts, that we may love all men and ever abide in peace and charity with all thy children. Bless all whom we love, and let thy mercies be upon all men, especially those who are afflicted; may their sorrows lead them to thee for comfort and salvation. Bless our home, and grant that it may ever be to us a type of that land where darkness and death come not. And when our course is ended here, may our whole family be reunited around thy throne in heaven. These mercies and blessings we ask in the name of Jesus Christ our Saviour. Amen.

III. LESSON. Isaiah liii.

Who hath believed our report? and to whom is the arm of the Lord revealed? For he shall grow up before him as a tender plant, and as a root out of a dry ground; he hath no form nor comeliness; and when we shall see him, there is no beauty that we should desire him. He is despised and rejected of men; a man of sorrows, and acquainted with grief; and we hid as it were our faces from him; he was despised, and we esteemed him not. Surely he hath borne our griefs, and carried our sorrows; yet we did esteem him stricken, smitten of God, and afflicted. But he was wounded for our transgressions, he was bruised for our iniquities; the chastisement of our peace was upon him; and with his stripes we are healed. All we like sheep have gone astray; we have turned every one to his own way; and the Lord hath laid on him the iniquity of us all. He was oppressed, and he was afflicted, yet he opened not his mouth; he is brought as a lamb to the slaughter, and as a sheep before her shearers is dumb, so he openeth not his mouth. He was taken from prison and from judgment; and who shall declare his generation? for he was cut off out of the land of the living; for the transgression of my people was he stricken. And he made his grave with the wicked, and with the rich in his death; because he had done no violence, neither was any deceit in his mouth. Yet it pleased the Lord to bruise him; he hath put him to grief; when thou shalt make his soul an offering for sin, he shall see his seed, he shall prolong his days, and the pleasure of the Lord shall prosper in his hand. He shall see of the travail of his soul, and shall be satisfied; by his knowledge shall my righteous servant justify many; for he shall bear their iniquities. Therefore will I divide him a portion with the great, and he shall divide the spoil with the strong; because he hath poured out his soul unto death; and he was numbered with the transgressors; and he bare the sin of many, and made intercession for the transgressors.

C. M.

Hosanna, with a cheerful sound,
  To God's upholding hand!
Ten thousand snares attend us round,
  And yet secure we stand.
God is our Sun, whose daily light
  Our joy and safety brings;
Our feeble flesh lies safe at night
  Beneath his shady wings.

PRAYER.

Our Father, we come to thee once more in thy appointed way. Breathe on us the Holy Spirit, that we may worship thee aright and bring thee an acceptable offering. Thy love has been shown unto us in very many ways. Not a moment to-day has failed to bring us blessings from thee, and thy unfailing goodness emboldens us to ask still greater blessings—even such blessings as only the all-powerful, all-wise, and all-loving God can give. Renewing our vows and reconsecrating ourselves to thy service, we pray that thou wilt pardon all that thou hast seen wrong in us to-day, and to make those wrongs so manifest unto us that we shall shun them in the days to come. Take care of us to-night, and defend us from every danger. Keep us in peace, whether we behold to-morrow's sun on earth or awake in heaven before the dawn. Bless the houseless and homeless to-night, and those who have no loving ones to pray for them. Bless those who are in the darkness and death of heathenism; and bless the missionaries whom thou hast sent to bear unto them the light and the life of the gospel of Christ. Bless the Board of Missions, and all thy people who are aiding in the extension of our Redeemer's kingdom.

Hasten the time when there shall be no more curse, and no night, and no death, and Christ shall be all and in all. Amen.

IV. LESSON. Deut. xxviii. 1-12.

AND it shall come to pass, if thou shalt hearken diligently unto the voice of the Lord thy God, to observe and to do all his commandments which I command thee this day, that the Lord thy God will set thee on high above all nations of the earth; and all these blessings shall come on thee, and overtake thee, if thou shalt hearken unto the voice of the Lord thy God. Blessed shalt thou be in the city, and blessed shalt thou be in the field. Blessed shall be the fruit of thy body, and the fruit of thy ground, and the fruit of thy cattle, the increase of thy kine, and the flocks of thy sheep. Blessed shall be thy basket and thy store. Blessed shalt thou be when thou comest in, and blessed shalt thou be when thou goest out. The Lord shall cause thine enemies that rise up against thee to be smitten before thy face; they shall come out against thee one way, and flee before thee seven ways. The Lord shall command the blessing upon thee in thy storehouses, and in all that thou settest thine hand unto; and he shall bless thee in the land which the Lord thy God giveth thee. The Lord shall establish thee a holy people unto himself, as he hath sworn unto thee, if thou shalt keep the commandments of the Lord thy God, and walk in his ways. And all people of the earth shall see that thou art called by the name of the Lord; and they shall be afraid of thee. And the Lord shall make thee plenteous in goods, in the fruit of thy body, and in the fruit of thy cattle, and in the fruit of thy ground, in the land which the Lord sware unto thy fathers to give thee. The Lord shall open unto thee his good treasure, the heaven to give the rain unto thy land in his season, and to bless all the work of thine hand; and thou shalt lend unto many nations, and thou shalt not borrow.

THE lines are fallen unto me in pleasant places; yea, I have a goodly heritage.

Psalm xvi. 6.

C. M.

How sweet and heavenly is the sight,
    When those that fear the Lord
In mutual love and peace delight,
    And thus fulfill his word!
When love in one delightful stream
    Through every bosom flows,
And union sweet, with fond esteem,
    In every action glows!

PRAYER.

Hear our prayer, O Lord; give ear to our supplications. In thy faithfulness answer us, and in thy righteousness; and enter not into judgment with thy servants, for in thy sight shall no man living be justified. Let our prayer be set forth before thee as incense, and the lifting up of our hands as the evening sacrifice. We would praise thee with our whole heart; we would worship toward thy holy temple, and praise thy name for thy loving-kindness and for thy truth; for thou hast magnified thy word above all thy name. Though thou art high, yet hast thou respect unto the lowly. Though we walk in the midst of trouble, thou wilt revive us. Thou wilt perfect that which concerneth us. Thy mercy, O Lord, endureth forever; forsake not the works of thine own hands. We bless thee that thou hast not forsaken us, but that through another day thou hast protected us from evil, and hast now brought us together around the family altar, to worship thee, our Father and our God. Enable us to worship thee in spirit and in truth, to offer thee our praises and our prayer through Jesus Christ our Lord. For his sake, accept our hearty thanks for all the mercies of the closing day, and for the blessings of our pilgrimage thus far; but most of all, for hope of endless life through him. Grant that we may from this time forth declare thy praise in all our conduct. May our behavior in all the relations of life be consistent with our high profession. In our daily intercourse with one another, may we be governed by a spirit of mutual sympathy and love. As parents, may we provoke not our children to wrath, but bring them up in thy nurture and admonition. As children, may we love one another, and obey our parents in all things. So likewise in our dealings with our fellow-men, may we have due regard to their interest and welfare. May we abhor that which is evil, and cleave to that which is good. May we be kindly affectioned one to another with brotherly love, in honor preferring one another, distributing to the necessity of saints, given to hospitality. May we recompense to no man evil for evil. May we provide things honest in the sight of all men. If it be possible, as much as lieth in us, may we live peaceably with all men. May we owe no man any thing, but to love one another. Most merciful Father, bless all for whom it is our duty now to pray. Smile on thy servants who are laboring to extend thy kingdom in the earth; on those who, having left their homes, are preaching Jesus and the resurrection in distant heathen lands; on all pious parents who by precept and example are training up their children in the way they should go; on earnest Christian workers in the Sunday-school, and on all faithful teachers of the young. And be merciful to the ungodly; to those who resist thy Spirit; to those who profane thy Sabbaths, and hallow not thy name; to those who defraud their fellow-men, and grind the face of the poor; to those who give their neighbors drink, and tempt the young to sin. Continue unto them thy grace, if even yet they may turn away from sin, and give themselves to thee. And now, Divine Protector, through the shades of night let thy strong wing be over us, that we may fear no evil, but rest secure in thee; that on the morrow we may rise refreshed, to spend the strength thou givest us in serving thee. And, when the night of death is past, raise us to everlasting life on high, through Jesus Christ our Lord. Amen.

For the upright shall dwell in the land, and the perfect shall remain in it. But the wicked shall be cut off from the earth, and the transgressors shall be rooted out of it.

Proverbs ii. 21, 22.

Services for Thursday Morning.

I. LESSON. Malachi iii. 1-12.

BEHOLD, I will send my messenger, and he shall prepare the way before me; and the Lord, whom ye seek, shall suddenly come to his temple, even the messenger of the covenant, whom ye delight in; behold, he shall come, saith the Lord of hosts. But who may abide the day of his coming? and who shall stand when he appeareth? for he is like a refiner's fire, and like fullers' soap; and he shall sit as a refiner and purifier of silver; and he shall purify the sons of Levi, and purge them as gold and silver, that they may offer unto the Lord an offering in righteousness. Then shall the offering of Judah and Jerusalem be pleasant unto the Lord, as in the days of old, and as in former years. And I will come near to you to judgment; and I will be a swift witness against the sorcerers, and against the adulterers, and against false swearers, and against those that oppress the hireling in his wages, the widow, and the fatherless, and that turn aside the stranger from his right, and fear not me, saith the Lord of hosts. For I am the Lord, I change not; therefore ye sons of Jacob are not consumed. Even from the days of your fathers ye are gone away from mine ordinances, and have not kept them. Return unto me, and I will return unto you, saith the Lord of hosts. But ye said, Wherein shall we return? Will a man rob God? Yet ye have robbed me. But ye say, Wherein have we robbed thee? In tithes and offerings. Ye are cursed with a curse; for ye have robbed me, even this whole nation. Bring ye all the tithes into the storehouse, that there may be meat in mine house, and prove me now herewith, saith the Lord of hosts, if I will not open you the windows of heaven, and pour you out a blessing, that there shall not be room enough to receive it. And I will rebuke the devourer for your sakes, and he shall not destroy the fruits of your ground; neither shall your vine cast her fruit before the time in the field, saith the Lord of hosts. And all nations shall call you blessed; for ye shall be a delightsome land, saith the Lord of hosts.

C. M.

Come, let us join our cheerful songs
    With angels round the throne:
Ten thousand thousand are their tongues,
    But all their joys are one.
"Worthy the Lamb that died!" they cry,
    "To be exalted thus."
"Worthy the Lamb," our hearts reply,
    For he was slain for us.

PRAYER.

Almighty God, our Heavenly Father, who art merciful and gracious, unto thee will we direct our prayer this morning, and will look up. We render hearty thanks unto thee for thy loving-kindness through another night, and for thy manifold and great mercies, which thou hast ever shown to us thy unworthy servants. We praise thee with all our souls for thy goodness and wonderful works to the children of men, and especially for the tokens of thy power, wisdom, and love, which we receive from thee day by day. O Lord, we are weak and sinful; thou art strong and mighty, infinitely holy, and filled with compassion for the sons of men; therefore draw near to us, even now, and help our prayer. Fill our souls with thy presence, and give to us continually such a deep sense of thy love for us, and such a yearning for things spiritual and heavenly, that we may have no taste for the pleasures of sin nor disposition to turn away from thee. We beseech thee for Jesus' sake that thou wilt take up thine abode with us; establish our souls in union and communion with thee; may our desires be holy, our thoughts pure and chaste, our wills submissive to thine, and our lives a sweet-smelling savor unto thee. Give to us strength of body and mind, wisdom and grace, that we may be able to perform the duties which we owe to thee, to our neighbors, and to one another. And now we commit ourselves into the keeping of the Father, the Son, and the Holy Ghost. O Lord, receive us, guide us by thy counsel, overshadow us with thy mercies continually; and may we live together in unity, peace, and happiness, through all our days. Amen.

II. LESSON. 2 Kings iv. 1-7.

Now there cried a certain woman of the wives of the sons of the prophets unto Elisha, saying, Thy servant my husband is dead; and thou knowest that thy servant did fear the Lord; and the creditor is come to take unto him my two sons to be bondmen. And Elisha said unto her, What shall I do for thee? tell me, what hast thou in the house? And she said, Thine handmaid hath not any thing in the house, save a pot of oil. Then he said, Go, borrow thee vessels abroad of all thy neighbors, even empty vessels; borrow not a few. And when thou art come in, thou shalt shut the door upon thee and upon thy sons, and shalt pour out into all those vessels, and thou shalt set aside that which is full. So she went from him, and shut the door upon her and upon her sons, who brought the vessels to her; and she poured out. And it came to pass, when the vessels were full, that she said unto her son, Bring me yet a vessel. And he said unto her, There is not a vessel more. And the oil staid. Then she came and told the man of God. And he said, Go, sell the oil, and pay thy debt, and live thou and thy children of the rest.

S. M.

Equip me for the war,
   And teach my hands to fight;
My simple, upright heart prepare,
   And guide my words aright.

PRAYER.

We thank thee, O Lord, that thou hast cared for us, and are glad that we know our blessings come from thee. We marvel that thou shouldst condescend to guide us in perplexity, make our bed in sickness, and guard us in the night season; but we are glad that we know it is so, and we pray thee to make us as grateful as we have been dependent. As we cannot profit thee by any service, nor enrich thee by our gifts, may we this day show our gratitude by our love and care for others. Help us to love, for thy sake, all men, even our enemies. Help us to be patient and tender and merciful, even as we are taught in thy word, remembering that we are called to this as children of the Highest. Help us to keep our tongues from evil, and our lips from speaking guile. May we be diligent in business and fervent in spirit. As we hope in thee, so may all thy promises be fulfilled in us; and may no trial be too great for our faith and patient endurance. If sorrows come, may they drive us to the cross for refuge; or if prosperity awaits us, may our hope of happiness not be based upon earthly things. Keep us from harm, and preserve us from dying unprepared to meet with God. Whatsoever we do, may it be done to the glory of God, so that in simplicity and godly sincerity we may have our conversation in the world. Whether we serve or suffer, may we therein be brought nearer to thee, so that when thy will has been accomplished here we may be received into thy kingdom above, where we will give thee perfect praise, through Christ our Lord. Amen.

III. LESSON. Luke xxiv. 1–9.

Now upon the first day of the week, very early in the morning, they came unto the sepulcher, bringing the spices which they had prepared, and certain others with them. And they found the stone rolled away from the sepulcher. And they entered in, and found not the body of the Lord Jesus. And it came to pass, as they were much perplexed thereabout, behold, two men stood by them in shining garments; and as they were afraid, and bowed down their faces to the earth, they said unto them, Why seek ye the living among the dead? He is not here, but is risen; remember how he spake unto you when he was yet in Galilee, saying, The Son of man must be delivered into the hands of sinful men, and be crucified, and the third day rise again. And they remembered his words, and returned from the sepulcher, and told all these things unto the eleven, and to all the rest.

L. M.

Just as I am—without one plea,
But that thy blood was shed for me,
And that thou bidst me come to thee—
  O Lamb of God, I come!

PRAYER.

O Lord, our Father, by whose tender care we have been preserved during another night, accept, we beseech thee, our morning service of praise and prayer. We thank thee for health and friends; for food, raiment, and for all other comforts of life: but above all we adore thee for sending thine only Son to redeem us from sin and eternal death. Keep us this day from sin, whether in thought, word, or deed. Remember us in mercy for our negligence and weakness. O make·us deeply to feel the evil of sin and the exceeding love of God; and may we earnestly endeavor, through thy grace assisting us, to follow the blessed precepts contained in the Holy Scriptures. May we take thy yoke upon us, and learn of thee, who art meek and lowly in heart, that we may find rest unto our souls. Hear our prayer, and grant us all things needful, we ask in the name of our Lord and Saviour Jesus Christ. Amen.

IV. LESSON. Isaiah xii.

AND in that day thou shalt say, O Lord, I will praise thee; though thou wast angry with me, thine anger is turned away, and thou comfortedst me. Behold, God is my salvation; I will trust and not be afraid; for the Lord Jehovah is my strength and my song; he also is become my salvation. Therefore with joy shall ye draw water out of the wells of salvation. And in that day shall ye say, Praise the Lord, call upon his name, declare his doings among the people, make mention that his name is exalted. Sing unto the Lord; for he hath done excellent things; this is known in all the earth. Cry out and shout, thou inhabitant of Zion; for great is the Holy One of Israel in the midst of thee.

C. M.

Lord, in the morning thou shalt hear
My voice ascending high;
To thee will I direct my prayer,
To thee lift up mine eye.

PRAYER.

Glory be to the Father, and to the Son, and to the Holy Ghost; as it was in the beginning, is now, and ever shall be, world without end. We bless thee, O Lord, the God of our salvation, who daily loadest us with benefits. Thou art the portion of our inheritance and of our cup. Thou maintainest our lot. The lines are fallen unto us in pleasant places: yea, we have a goodly heritage. We thank thee for conjugal esteem, for parental love, for filial affection, for fraternal harmony, for social good, for general welfare. We do trace our every blessing unto thee, O Father of lights, with whom is no variableness, neither shadow of turning. Thou hast preserved us through another night. While we lay wrapped in sleep, unconscious of our very being, thy sleepless care defended us from harm, and kept our dwelling safe from all calamity. And now, restored to life, and strengthened by repose, we enter on the duties of the day, by meeting in thy name to give thee thanks for all the past, and ask thy blessing on our future lives. We know that we cannot succeed in any thing without thy help and blessing. And we beseech thee now to help us in our work this day, that in our honest efforts to cultivate ourselves, and to improve our lot in life, we may have such success as it shall please thee to bestow. To this end give us a spirit of industry, that we may love our work, and feel that as we labor in our several callings we are doing thy will concerning us. And may we never try to do any thing that thou wilt not approve. Thou Giver of every good and perfect gift, give us a spirit of liberality. Help us to bear in mind that all we have is thine. May we respond with gladness to every worthy call of human need or Christian enterprise; that by our personal service, or by gifts of money, as thou hast prospered us, we may relieve distressed humanity, and spread thy kingdom in the earth. Enable us to avoid all dissipation, extravagance, intemperance, and excess. May our moderation be known unto all men. May we be careful for nothing, but in every thing by prayer and supplication with thanksgiving let our requests be made known unto thee. May we learn in whatsoever state we are therewith to be content. And may thy peace, which passeth all understanding, keep our hearts and minds, through Christ Jesus. We now commend to thine almighty care all those who, distant from us in the flesh, are dear to us at heart. Be with them in their wanderings or in their homes, as they may roam or rest. Grant them thy peace and help, as may be best for them; and as in love and wisdom thou shalt sometimes disappoint their hopes, or send them real affliction, enable them to feel that even then thou doest all things well. Be merciful to all mankind, especially to those who suffer. Lift up those who are bowed down, succor the tempted, heal the sick, strengthen the weak, and comfort those who mourn thy love to know. Again we ask thy blessing on our work this day. Give us wisdom from on high for every duty. Continue to us evermore thy guidance and protection; and when our work is done below, receive us to thyself above, for our Redeemer's sake. Amen.

Services for Thursday Evening.

I. LESSON.   Luke iv. 1-13.

AND Jesus being full of the Holy Ghost returned from Jordan, and was led by the Spirit into the wilderness, being forty days tempted of the devil. And in those days he did eat nothing; and when they were ended, he afterward hungered. And the devil said unto him, If thou be the Son of God, command this stone that it be made bread. And Jesus answered him, saying, It is written, That man shall not live by bread alone, but by every word of God. And the devil, taking him up into a high mountain, shewed unto him all the kingdoms of the world in a moment of time. And the devil said unto him, All this power will I give thee, and the glory of them; for that is delivered unto me; and to whomsoever I will, I give it. If thou therefore wilt worship me, all shall be thine. And Jesus answered and said unto him, Get thee behind me, Satan; for it is written, Thou shalt worship the Lord thy God, and him only shalt thou serve. And he brought him to Jerusalem, and set him on a pinnacle of the temple, and said unto him, If thou be the Son of God, cast thyself down from hence; for it is written, He shall give his angels charge over thee, to keep thee; and in their hands they shall bear thee up, lest at any time thou dash thy foot against a stone. And Jesus answering said unto him, It is said, Thou shalt not tempt the Lord thy God. And when the devil had ended all the temptation, he departed from him for a season.

L. M.

Thus far the Lord hath led me on,
　Thus far his power prolongs my days,
And every evening shall make known
　Some fresh memorial of his grace.
I lay my body down to sleep,
　Peace is the pillow for my head;
While well-appointed angels keep
　Their watchful stations round my bed.

PRAYER.

Our Heavenly Father, thou hast kindly cared for us during the day now just gone, and we give thee heart-felt thanks for all thy blessings. Thou didst graciously guide us through the hours since morning, and didst help us in the duties and perplexities of life. Now we pray that thou wouldst forgive us whatever we have thought or felt or said or done that was wrong in thy sight, and give us the blessing of that peace and mercy which thou dost bestow for

Jesus' sake. May we truly love and trust thee this night, and may we cast all our care upon thee, because thou carest for us. We would be as little children, under the protection of our wise and good Heavenly Father, and we pray that thy loving-kindness may give us such rest in sleep as may be needed for our further duties and labors in life on to-morrow. May each day and night of our future time be so employed as to result in greater good to our fellow-men and higher glory to thy great name than the past has accomplished. We earnestly pray for due preparation to meet thee in peace in the great day of thy power, and to be kept in the love and favor of Christ always unto everlasting life. We are thine in "spirit and soul and body," and we ask that we may be consecrated to thy service in worship and work forever and ever. Amen.

II. LESSON. Luke i. 68-79.

BLESSED be the Lord God of Israel; for he hath visited and redeemed his people, and hath raised up a horn of salvation for us in the house of his servant David; as he spake by the mouth of his holy prophets, which have been since the world began; that we should be saved from our enemies, and from the hand of all that hate us; to perform the mercy promised to our fathers, and to remember his holy covenant; the oath which he sware to our father Abraham, that he would grant unto us, that we, being delivered out of the hand of our enemies, might serve him without fear, in holiness and righteousness before him, all the days of our life. And thou, child, shalt be called the prophet of the Highest; for thou shalt go before the face of the Lord to prepare his ways; to give knowledge of salvation unto his people by the remission of their sins, through the tender mercy of our God; whereby the day-spring from on high hath visited us, to give light to them that sit sin darkness and in the shadow of death, to guide our feet into the way of peace.

I WILL both lay me down in peace, and sleep; for thou, Lord, only makest me dwell in safety.
Psalm iv. 8.

7s.
OMNIPRESENT God! whose aid
   No one ever asked in vain,
Be this night about my bed,
   Every evil thought restrain:
Lay thy hand upon my soul,
   God of my unguarded hours!
All my enemies control,
   Hell, and earth, and nature's powers.

PRAYER.

O MERCIFUL God, thou art our Father, and we are thy children by faith in Jesus Christ; let thy loving mercy and tender compassion descend upon us this evening. As we bow before thee, we lift our hearts to thee in praise, thanksgiving, and adoration for the many blessings which thou hast granted unto us through the day. Thou hast been our guardian and guide, our light and our salvation, and now, around our family altar, we commit our souls and bodies into thy gracious care and keeping, begging thee for thy mercy and protection through the night. Bless all whom we love, and all who love us, even as we ask thee to bless ourselves. O Lord, with sad hearts we think of our misdoings this day. We confess our sins against thee; the remembrance of them is grievous unto us; but thou art the God of mercy, and willing to forgive all who call upon thee. Have mercy upon us; for Jesus' sake blot out our sins, and remember them against us no more forever. O Lord, how frail we are, how weak and sinful; exposed to temptations, and not able of ourselves to resist them. Strengthen us by thy Holy Spirit that we may be able to resist evil, to do justly, to love mercy, and to walk humbly with thee all our days. Amen.

III. LESSON. Matthew xvii. 1-8.

AND after six days, Jesus taketh Peter, James, and John his brother, and bringeth them up into a high mountain apart, and was transfigured before them; and his face did shine as the sun, and his raiment was white as the light. And, behold, there appeared unto them Moses and Elias talking with him. Then answered Peter, and said unto Jesus, Lord, it is good for us to be here; if thou wilt, let us make here three tabernacles; one for thee, and one for Moses, and one for Elias. While he yet spake, behold, a bright cloud overshadowed them; and behold a voice out of the cloud, which said, This is my beloved Son, in whom I am well pleased; hear ye him. And when the disciples heard it, they fell on their face, and were sore afraid. And Jesus came and touched them, and said, Arise, and be not afraid.

7s.

LET me of thy life partake,
  Thy own holiness impart;
O that I may sweetly wake,
  With my Saviour in my heart!
O that I may know thee mine!
  O that I may thee receive!
Only live the life divine!
  Only to thy glory live.

PRAYER.

O Lord, we acknowledge thee in all our ways. We bow down at the close of this day to offer our sacrifice of praise and thanksgiving. Hear our prayer, O Lord, and give ear to our supplication. We confess our unworthiness, and the sense of our ingratitude is painful unto us. We pray thee have mercy upon us, and forgive all our sins, and remove our iniquities far from us. May we lie down this night feeling that we are reconciled unto thee, and that we are accepted of thee through Jesus Christ. Be pleased, O Lord, to defend against fire and pestilence and sickness and sudden death. May no plague come nigh our dwelling. We are reminded that the night cometh when no man can work. Our days are but as a shadow upon the earth. Help us that we may apply ourselves with diligence to every good work and serve thy righteous will continually. Grant unto us, O Lord, spiritual-mindedness and a continual growth in grace. And may we so live in this world that, having served our day and generation, by the will of God, we may finally rest with thee through Jesus Christ our Lord. Amen.

The wicked flee when no man pursueth; but the righteous are bold as a lion. Proverbs xxviii, 1.

IV. LESSON. Colossians iii. 12-25.

Put on therefore, as the elect of God, holy and beloved, bowels of mercies, kindness, humbleness of mind, meekness, long-suffering; forbearing one another, and forgiving one another, if any man have a quarrel against any; even as Christ forgave you, so also do ye. And above all these things put on charity, which is the bond of perfectness. And let the peace of God rule in your hearts, to the which also ye are called in one body; and be ye thankful. Let the word of Christ dwell in you richly in all wisdom; teaching and admonishing one another in psalms and hymns and spiritual songs, singing with grace in your hearts to the Lord. And whatsoever ye do in word or deed, do all in the name of the Lord Jesus, giving thanks to God and the Father by him. Wives, submit yourselves unto your own husbands, as it is fit in the Lord. Husbands, love your wives, and be not bitter against them. Children, obey your parents in all things; for this is well-pleasing unto the Lord. Fathers, provoke not your children to anger, lest they be discouraged. Servants, obey in all things your masters according to the flesh; not with eye-service, as men-pleasers; but in singleness of heart, fearing God; and whatsoever ye do, do it heartily, as to the Lord, and not unto men; knowing that of the Lord ye shall receive the reward of the inheritance; for ye serve the Lord Christ. But he that doeth wrong shall receive for the wrong which he hath done; and there is no respect of persons.

L. M.

Lord, how secure and blessed are they
　Who feel the joys of pardoned sin!
Should storms of wrath shake earth and sea,
　Their minds have heaven and peace within.

The day glides sweetly o'er their heads,
　Made up of innocence and love;
And soft and silent as the shades
　Their nightly minutes gently move.

PRAYER.

As now again, O Lord, the shades of night have gathered around us, we come together as a Christian house, to offer up our evening sacrifice to thee. Help us to worship thee in spirit and in truth, that in response to our devotions offered through our Saviour Jesus Christ we may receive the blessings that we need for this life and in reference to the life which is to come. We come to thank thee for the special mercies of another day. While many of our fellow-beings entered on the day with hopes as bright as ours, they have been suddenly cut off, and are now testing the realities of the unseen world. While others have been tossed in pain on beds of suffering, we have had health and strength for duty all the day. And now as we enjoy the comforts of our happy home, with food and raiment and all things needed for our mutual joy, many are wearing out their wretched lives in the bitterness and woe of friendless poverty. O Lord, we are not worthy of the least of all the mercies, and of all the truth, which thou hast shown unto thy servants; for our transgressions are multiplied before thee, and our sins testify against us. What shall we render unto thee for all thy benefits toward us? We will take the cup of salvation, and call upon thy holy name. We will offer to thee the sacrifice of thanksgiving, and tell of all thy wondrous works. Not with our lips alone, O Father, but in our lives as well, would we show forth thy praise. We would be led by thy countless mercies to present our bodies a living sacrifice, holy, acceptable unto thee, which is our reasonable service; and being not conformed to this world, we would be transformed by the renewing of our mind, that we may prove what is that good and acceptable and perfect will of thine. We would not think of ourselves more highly than we ought to think, but soberly, according as thou hast dealt to every one the measure of faith. We would bear in mind that to whom much is given of him is much required; and as we have received unusual favor from thy hand, so would we strive in every way to requite thy goodness with humble obedience, as well as gratitude and love. Look down with favor, Heavenly Father, on all the efforts of thy people to elevate and bless humanity, and extend the influence of thy kingdom in the earth. Give wisdom and zeal to those who are charged with the training of the young at home and in school. May they cultivate the affections as well as the minds and manners of those intrusted to their care, that teachers and taught may together learn from thee the heavenly lessons of thy love. Bless the conductors of the press, both secular and religious. May they not pander to the tastes of the ungodly, but keep out of their columns all that would tend to degrade and corrupt the public heart; and may their great power be always used on the side of virtue and truth. Restrain the reckless wickedness of those who, in their hot pursuit of gain, would rouse the baser passions of mankind, by selling impure books or papers, by leading others into dens of shame, by deceiving the simple in gambling-saloons, by putting the bottle to their neighbors' lips. Against all such devices of the wicked one wilt thou, O Lord, arouse the public conscience, that all our virtuous people may rise in their might, and by ceaseless and united effort drive them forever from our happy land. And now, O Heavenly Father, we lay ourselves with all our interests and cares, in quiet confidence within thy hollow hand. During our sleeping hours be our defense; and sleeping or awake, be still our portion now and evermore. Amen.

For my loins are filled with a loathsome disease; and there is no soundness in my flesh. I am feeble and sore broken; I have roared by reason of the disquietness of my heart. Lord, all my desire is before thee; and my groaning is not hid from thee. My heart panteth, my strength faileth me; as for the light of mine eyes, it also is gone from me. My lovers and my friends stand aloof from my sore; and my kinsmen stand afar off. Forsake me not, O Lord; O my God, be not far from me. Make haste to help me, O Lord my salvation.

Psalm xxxviii. 7–11, 21, 22.

Services for Friday Morning.

I. LESSON. Luke vii. 19-23.

AND John calling unto him two of his disciples sent them to Jesus, saying, Art thou he that should come? or look we for another? When the men were come unto him, they said, John Baptist hath sent us unto thee, saying, Art thou he that should come? or look we for another? And in that same hour he cured many of their infirmities and plagues, and of evil spirits; and unto many that were blind he gave sight. Then Jesus answering said unto them, Go your way, and tell John what things ye have seen and heard; how that the blind see, the lame walk, the lepers are cleansed, the deaf hear, the dead are raised, to the poor the gospel is preached. And blessed is he whosoever shall not be offended in me.

S. M.

WE lift our hearts to thee,
  O Day-star from on high!
The sun itself is but thy shade,
  Yet cheers both earth and sky.

May we this life improve,
  To mourn for errors past;
And live this short revolving day
  As if it were our last.

FRIDAY MORNING.

PRAYER.

Our Father and our God, we are grateful to thee for thy goodness and thy wonderful works. Day by day have our wants been supplied, and night by night have thy mercies been bestowed. "Surely goodness and mercy have followed" us all our days, and we hope to "dwell in the house of the Lord forever." And now we come to thee once more, asking pardon for all the errors and sins of the past. If our penitence be not deep enough nor our faith strong enough to meet the conditions of thy grace, then we beseech thee deepen thy work in our hearts until we hate sin and turn from evil and look unto Jesus, our only hope and our God. Give unto us the witness of thy Spirit. Bless not only us who are here bowed in thy presence, but also our absent loved ones. Guide our steps, uphold us with thy power, comfort us with thy love, and establish thou the work of our hands. Keep us in the path of duty, and help us to do something in the cause of Christ this day. Bless our community, and keep far from us all pestilence and plague and famine. Revive thy work in our midst; convict sinners, comfort mourners, consecrate believers, and help thy people to be earnest, zealous, and true. Amen.

II. LESSON. Proverbs xi. 17-31.

THE merciful man doeth good to his own soul; but he that is cruel troubleth his own flesh. The wicked worketh a deceitful work; but to him that soweth righteousness shall be a sure reward. As righteousness tendeth to life, so he that pursueth evil pursueth it to his own death. They that are of a froward heart are abomination to the Lord; but such as are upright in their way are his delight. Though hand join in hand, the wicked shall not be unpunished; but the seed of the righteous shall be delivered. As a jewel of gold in a swine's snout, so is a fair woman which is without discretion. The desire of the righteous is only good; but the expectation of the wicked is wrath. There is that scattereth, and yet increaseth; and there is that withholdeth more than is meet, but it tendeth to poverty. The liberal soul shall be made fat; and he that watereth shall be watered also himself. He that withholdeth corn, the people shall curse him; but blessing shall be upon the head of him that selleth it. He that diligently seeketh good procureth favor; but he that seeketh mischief, it shall come unto him. He that trusteth in his riches shall fall; but the righteous shall flourish as a branch. He that troubleth his own house shall inherit the wind; and the fool shall be servant to the wise of heart. The fruit of the righteous is a tree of life; and he that winneth souls is wise. Behold, the righteous shall be recompensed in the earth; much more the wicked and the sinner.

O THAT men would praise the Lord for his goodness, and for his wonderful works to the children of men! Psalm cvii. 8.

S. M.
TEACH me, my God and King,
In all things thee to see;
And what I do, in any thing,
To do it as for thee;

To scorn the senses' sway,
While still to thee I tend:
In all I do be thou the way,
In all be thou the end.

PRAYER.

ALMIGHTY GOD, our Heavenly Father, we thank thee for the morning light and for thy loving-kindness unto us. Every day brings some new display of thy love and favor, so that we are led to acknowledge our entire dependence upon thee. It is with shame and confusion that we remember our unworthiness in thy sight. O Lord, we make our humble confession before thee. Hear our prayer, and deal with us, not according to our righteousness, but according to thy great mercy, O blessed Lord God. Continue thy tender mercies toward us this day, and lead us by the Holy Spirit into plain and safe paths. Deliver us from every vain and wicked imagination, and from an ungodly temper and from all uncharitable and unprofitable conversation. In every hour of trial and severe temptation stand by us and support us by thy grace. May we never fall from thee! Give unto us patience in all seasons of sickness, and may we be perfectly resigned to thy holy will in all things. Grant unto us, O Lord, the spirit of prayer continually, that we may abound yet more and more in the fruits of the Spirit. Illumine our minds, that we may have a right understanding in the things of life, and that we may shun every evil way. And comfort us with thy holy presence continually. If thou shouldst be pleased to prosper us in business, keep us back from covetousness and from pride and from vanity; and help us, O Lord, that we may live soberly and righteously in this present world, and finally come to the land of everlasting life, there to reign with thee world without end. Amen.

III. LESSON. Matthew xviii. 1-14.

AT the same time came the disciples unto Jesus, saying, Who is the greatest in the kingdom of heaven? And Jesus called a little child unto him, and set him in the midst of them, and said, Verily I say unto you, Except ye be converted, and become as little children, ye shall not enter into the kingdom of heaven. Whosoever therefore shall humble himself as this little child, the same is greatest in the kingdom of heaven. And whoso shall receive one such little child in my name receiveth me. But whoso shall offend one of these little ones which believe in me, it were better for him that a millstone were hanged about his neck, and that he were drowned in the depth of the sea. Woe unto the world because of offenses! for it must needs be that offenses come; but woe to that man by whom the offense cometh! Wherefore, if thy hand or thy foot offend thee, cut them off, and cast them from thee; it is better for thee to enter into life halt or maimed, rather than having two hands or two feet to be cast into everlasting fire. And if thine eye offend thee, pluck it out, and cast it from thee; it is better for thee to enter into life with one eye, rather than having two eyes to be cast into hell-fire. Take heed that ye despise not one of these little ones; for I say unto you, That in heaven their angels do always behold the face of my Father which is in heaven. For the Son of man is come to save that which was lost. How think ye? if a man have a hundred sheep, and one of them be gone astray, doth he not leave the ninety and nine, and goeth into the mountains, and seeketh that which is gone astray? And if so be that he find it, verily I say unto you, he rejoiceth more of that sheep, than of the ninety and nine which went not astray. Even so it is not the will of your Father which is in heaven, that one of these little ones should perish.

———

He that, being often reproved, hardeneth his neck, shall suddenly be destroyed, and that without remedy. — Proverbs xxix. 1.

S. M.

Serene I laid me down,
  Beneath his guardian care;
I slept, and I awoke, and found
  My kind Preserver near.

My life I would anew
  Devote, O Lord, to thee;
And in thy service I would spend
  A long eternity.

PRAYER.

O LORD, in the name of Jesus we come to thee this morning in prayer and praise. We thank thee for our safety and rest during the past night, and for the many blessings which we now enjoy. "Every good gift and every perfect gift is from above, and cometh down from the Father of lights." We acknowledge our entire dependence on thee for all good, temporal and spiritual. Grant that we may this day be sensible of thy providential care over us, and may we heartily feel the need and the blessing of thy saving grace. We are prone to forget the goodness of God, and we pray that our weak and erring hearts may be kept from too great temptation to neglect of duty. We need the enlightening and sanctifying influence of the Holy Spirit, and we ask that it may be bestowed upon us in liberal measure. O teach us more and more perfectly thy will and ways, and enable us to walk in, them in the obedience of true faith, with humility and sincerity. Help us to spend this day so that we may glorify thy name in all things. Grant that we may be "not slothful in business, fervent in spirit, serving the Lord, rejoicing in hope, patient in tribulation, continuing instant in prayer." May we be useful to each other, and to other persons in the duties and labors of life, showing a gentle spirit of forbearance and a wise zeal in work. As peculiar trials may come to us, may especial grace be afforded at such times of need, and may we be only better fitted to serve thee by the hardships we may suffer. Grant that we may grow wiser and stronger and better in preparation for the life to come, and at last save us in heaven, for Jesus' sake. Amen.

IV. LESSON. John iii. 1-16.

THERE was a man of the Pharisees, named Nicodemus, a ruler of the Jews; the same came to Jesus by night, and said unto him, Rabbi, we know that thou art a teacher come from God; for no man can do these miracles that thou doest, except God be with him. Jesus answered and said unto him, Verily, verily, I say unto thee, Except a man be born again, he cannot see the kingdom of God. Nicodemus saith unto him, How can a man be born when he is old? can he enter the second time into his mother's womb, and be born? Jesus answered, Verily, verily, I say unto thee, Except a man be born of water and of the Spirit, he cannot enter into the kingdom of heaven. That which is born of the flesh is flesh; and that which is born of the Spirit is spirit. Marvel not that I said unto thee, Ye must be born again. The wind bloweth where it listeth, and thou hearest the sound thereof, but canst not tell whence it cometh, and whither it goeth; so is every one that is born of the Spirit. Nicodemus answered and said unto him, How can these things be? Jesus answered and said unto him, Art thou a master of Israel, and knowest not these things? Verily, verily, I say unto thee, We speak that we do know, and testify that we have seen; and ye receive not our witness. If I have told you earthly things, and ye believe not, how shall ye believe, if I tell you of heavenly things? And no man hath ascended up to heaven, but he that came down from heaven, even the Son of man which is in heaven. And as Moses lifted up the serpent in the wilderness, even so must the Son of man be lifted up; that whosoever believeth in him should not perish, but have eternal life. For God so loved the world, that he gave his only begotten Son, that whosoever believeth in him should not perish, but have everlasting life.

7s.

Lord, we come before thee now,
  At thy feet we humbly bow;
O do not our suit disdain:
  Shall we seek thee, Lord, in vain?

PRAYER.

Lord, thou hast been our dwelling-place in all generations. Before the mountains were brought forth or ever thou hadst formed the earth and the world, even from everlasting to everlasting, thou art God. Thou turnest man to destruction, and sayest, Return, ye children of men. For a thousand years in thy sight are but as yesterday when it is past, and as a watch in the night. The days of our years are three-score years and ten; and, if by reason of strength they be four-score years, yet is their strength labor and sorrow; for it is soon cut off, and we fly away. So teach us to number our days that we may apply our hearts unto wisdom. We adore thee that, though thou art of purer eyes than to behold evil, and canst not look on iniquity, thou didst send thy Son into the world, not to condemn the world, but that the world through him might be saved. And thou commendest thy love toward us, in that, while we were yet sinners, Christ died for us. Help us this Friday morning, Heavenly Father, to celebrate his dying love. Enable us by faith to gaze upon his agony and bloody sweat; to see his base betrayal to the Jewish mob; to follow him in sad devotion from the garden to the palace; and, after hearing all the charges falsely brought against him, may we, like Pilate, find no fault in him at all. Help us by faith with Simon to relieve his weary frame by carrying his cross to Calvary; and, as we see him hanging there in agony and blood, and feel that our sins helped to nail him there, O may we hear his dying prayer for us, "Father, forgive them; for they know not what they do." Grant us, O Lord, to see in his bitter sufferings and cruel death both how thou hatest sin, and how thou lovest sinful men. And, as we mourn in earnest anguish our fallen nature, our evil tendencies, our wicked deeds, our sinful habits, may we take courage from the fact that through the redemption that is in his death thou mayest be just and the justifier of him which believeth in Jesus. Lord, we believe; help thou our unbelief. Strengthen our faith in thee; that, being justified by faith, we may have peace with thee through our Lord Jesus Christ, by whom also we have access by faith into this grace wherein we stand, and rejoice in the hope of thy coming glory. As we enter now upon the duties of the day, enable us to bear in mind the debt of gratitude we owe to thee for all the benefits and blessings of the new and everlasting covenant. In all our dealings with our fellow-men may we show forth thy praise by doing only such things as thou wilt smile upon and approve. May we set before others examples worthy of their imitation, and by every practicable means induce them to be faithful in thy service. And, if it please thee, may we succeed in pointing some wretched sinner to the fountain opened to the house of David for sin and for uncleanness. Look mercifully, O Lord, this day on all thine earthly creatures. According to their varied needs grant them the blessings of thy providence and grace. Prosper every honest effort to extend the kingdom of thy Son. Dispose the hearts of sinful men to accept the terms of the gospel. Stir up thy followers to diligence in duty. Lift up those that are bowed down under manifold temptations. Give comfort to all who suffer. Relieve the distresses of the needy. Mitigate the sorrows of those whom thou hast recently bereaved. Give courage and triumph to those who are called to die. Hear us, O Heavenly Father, in these our humble prayers, and grant us answers of peace and joy, through Jesus Christ our Lord. Amen.

My voice shalt thou hear in the morning, O Lord; in the morning will I direct my prayer unto thee, and will look up. Psalm v. 3.

Services for Friday Evening.

I. LESSON. Psalm xv.

LORD, who shall abide in thy tabernacle? who shall dwell in thy holy hill? He that walketh uprightly, and worketh righteousness, and speaketh the truth in his heart. He that backbiteth not with his tongue, nor doeth evil to his neighbor, nor taketh up a reproach against his neighbor. In whose eyes a vile person is contemned; but he honoreth them that fear the Lord. He that sweareth to his own hurt, and changeth not. He that putteth not out his money to usury, nor taketh reward against the innocent. He that doeth these things shall never be moved.

HE that loveth pleasure shall be a poor man; he that loveth wine and oil shall not be rich.

Proverbs xxi. 17.

C. M.

O FOR a lowly, contrite heart,
  Believing, true, and clean!
Which neither death nor life can part
  From Him that dwells within:

A heart in every thought renewed,
  And full of love divine;
Perfect, and right, and pure, and good—
  A copy, Lord, of thine.

PRAYER.

ALMIGHTY GOD, our Heavenly Father, we come to this evening hour of devotion realizing our sinfulness and our unworthiness. We come in the name of Jesus Christ, pleading the merits of his death, throwing ourselves upon thy compassions, which fail not. We pray for pardon and peace and reconciliation, through our Lord Jesus Christ. We pray that we may be accepted of God, and adopted into the family of heaven. Forgive us for any thing wrong in any of us during the day. Record thy name with us, and come unto us from time to time, and bless us. We commit and commend ourselves unto our faithful covenant-keeping God for the night. Watch over us with parental care; keep away from us and our home disease and danger and death. Give us rest in sleep. Bring us, O Lord, to the light of another day, with such blessings as thou seest will be for our good. Bless us in the relations we sustain each to the other, in the relations we sustain to the Church, and all others. Guide us with thy counsel. Bless us with thy presence. Prepare us for all the duties of life. Reconcile us to the dispensations of thy providence, and save us together in heaven, through Jesus Christ our Redeemer. Amen.

II. LESSON. Heb. xii. 1–17.

WHEREFORE, seeing we also are compassed about with so great a cloud of witnesses, let us lay aside every weight, and the sin which doth so easily beset us, and let us run with patience the race that is set before us, looking unto Jesus the author and finisher of our faith; who for the joy that was set before him endured the cross, despising the shame, and is set down at the right-hand of the throne of God. For consider him that endureth such contradiction of sinners against himself, lest ye be wearied and faint in your minds. Ye have not yet resisted unto blood, striving against sin. And ye have forgotten the exhortation which speaketh unto you as unto children, My son, despise not thou the chastening of the Lord, nor faint when thou art rebuked of him; for whom the Lord loveth he chasteneth, and scourgeth every son whom he receiveth. If ye endure chastening, God dealeth with you as with sons; for what son is he whom the father chasteneth not? But if ye be without chastisement, whereof all are partakers, then are ye bastards, and not sons. Furthermore, we have had fathers of our flesh which corrected us, and we gave them reverence; shall we not much rather be in subjection unto the Father of spirits, and live? For they verily for a few days chastened us after their own pleasure; but he for our profit, that we might be partakers of his holiness. Now no chastening for the present seemeth to be joyous, but grievous; nevertheless, afterward it yieldeth the peaceable fruit of righteousness unto them which are exercised thereby. Wherefore lift up the hands which hang down, and the feeble knees; and make straight paths for your feet, lest that which is lame be turned out of the way; but let it rather be healed. Follow peace with all men, and holiness, without which no man shall see the Lord; looking diligently lest any man fail of the grace of God; lest any root of bitterness springing up trouble you, and thereby many be defiled; lest there be any fornicator, or profane person, as Esau, who for one morsel of meat sold his birthright. For ye know how that afterward, when he would have inherited the blessing, he was rejected; for he found no place of repentance, though he sought it carefully with tears.

L. M.
Just as I am—thy love unknown
Has broken every barrier down;
Now to be thine, yea, thine alone,
  O Lamb of God, I come!

PRAYER.

At thy feet, O Lord, we bow in humble and grateful acknowledgments of the mercies of another day. We bless thee for the power that hath protected us, the wisdom that hath guided us, the bounty that hath fed us, the mercy that hath borne with us. We thank thee for the means of grace and for the hope of glory, and would close this day marked by thy unfailing yet unmerited goodness by joining our hearts and our voices in praises to thy holy name. Graciously pardon all our misdoings and short-comings, O Lord; help us to rest in unwavering faith in the atoning blood of the Son of God, who loved us and gave himself for us; and as the holy quiet of the night falls upon the natural world, wrapped in darkness and silence, so may thy peace, O blessed Father in heaven, rest upon our believing, loving hearts as we lay us down upon our beds to sleep. Thy wisdom hath guided us through the day; so may thy power protect us through the night. So we will both lay us down and sleep; for thou, Lord, only makest us dwell in safety. Mercifully guide, bless, and keep us through all our days of toil and nights of rest or of pain and sorrow; and bring us, each and all, when the night of death shall come, to be ready as servants that wait for their Lord, that in the morning of the resurrection we may awake in his likeness and be satisfied. Amen.

III. LESSON. Proverbs xxvii. 1-12.

Boast not thyself of to-morrow; for thou knowest not what a day may bring forth. Let another man praise thee, and not thine own mouth; a stranger, and not thine own lips. A stone is heavy, and the sand weighty, but a fool's wrath is heavier than them both. Wrath is cruel, and anger is outrageous; but who is able to stand before envy? Open rebuke is better than secret love. Faithful are the wounds of a friend; but the kisses of an enemy are deceitful. The full soul loatheth a honey-comb; but to the hungry soul every bitter thing is sweet. As a bird that wandereth from her nest, so is a man that wandereth from his place. Ointment and perfume rejoice the heart; so doth the sweetness of a man's friend by hearty counsel. Thine own friend, and thy father's friend, forsake not; neither go into thy brother's house in the day of thy calamity; for better is a neighbor that is near than a brother far off. My son, be wise, and make my heart glad, that I may answer him that reproacheth me. A prudent man foreseeth the evil, and hideth himself; but the simple pass on, and are punished.

7s.

Grant that all may seek and find
Thee a gracious God, and kind;
Heal the sick, the captive free;
Let us all rejoice in thee.

PRAYER.

Almighty and most merciful Father, we come to render thanks for the mercies of another day, and to implore thy care and blessing for the night. Give us rest from toil, and from every evil thought. Preserve us from the pestilence that walketh in darkness and from the destruction that wasteth at noonday. Take this house and every inmate of it under thy gracious protection. May we lie down at peace with thee. We have not served thee this day nor loved thee as we ought. For Jesus' sake forgive us all that is past, and in future life give us grace to work before thee in love. Bless with us all whom we love and all who love us, all to whom we are indebted for any help or comfort. Look in mercy upon the earth which thou hast made and upon all the sorrows of thy creatures, and turn their thoughts to thee as the God of grace and the giver of every good and perfect gift. Bless thy Church universal, and make it the joy of the whole earth. Ever be our God and guide, and save us in thy kingdom, for Jesus' sake. Amen.

IV. LESSON. Proverbs x. 1-12.

The Proverbs of Solomon. A wise son maketh a glad father; but a foolish son is the heaviness of his mother. The treasures of wickedness profit nothing; but righteousness delivereth from death. The Lord will not suffer the soul of the righteous to famish; but he casteth away the substance of the wicked. He becometh poor that dealeth with a slack hand; but the hand of the diligent maketh rich. He that gathereth in summer is a wise son; but he that sleepeth in harvest is a son that causeth shame. Blessings are upon the head of the just; but violence covereth the mouth of the wicked. The memory of the just is blessed; but the name of the wicked shall rot. The wise in heart will receive commandments; but a prating fool shall fall. He that walketh uprightly walketh surely; but he that perverteth his ways shall be known. He that winketh with the eye causeth sorrow; but a prating fool shall fall. The mouth of a righteous man is a well of life; but violence covereth the mouth of the wicked. Hatred stirreth up strifes; but love covereth all sins.

C. M.

O FOR a heart to praise my God,
  A heart from sin set free!
A heart that always feels thy blood
  So freely spilt for me!

A heart resigned, submissive, meek,
  My great Redeemer's throne,
Where only Christ is heard to speak,
  Where Jesus reigns alone.

PRAYER.

HELP us, O Lord, our Father and our God, to worship thee to-night in spirit and in truth. Grant us thy Spirit to teach us how to pray, that our devotions offered in the name of Jesus Christ thy Son may be acceptable to thee, and may result in blessings from thy hand precisely suited to our several needs. Grant us a spirit of earnest gratitude to thee for all the mercies thou hast furnished us through all our lives. May we believe and feel that every comfort we enjoy comes down from thee, and that without thy constant care we would be instantly destroyed. May we rejoice in the fact that thus far thou hast caused all things to work together for our good. Give us a spirit of sweet submission to thy holy will. May we feel that we are not capable of choosing for ourselves or knowing what is best for us; and when from time to time thou seest fit to disappoint our hopes and blast our cherished plans, may we in every case without a murmur yield to thy superior wisdom, and adore thy fatherly love. And give us a spirit of active industry in thy cause. May we desire to be about our Heavenly Father's business. May love to thee and love for all mankind induce us to exert ourselves in every proper way to help and bless our fellows and to glorify thy name. Thou knowest, O Father, how imperfectly we have served thee since we professed thy name. Like Peter, we have too often followed thee at a distance. Even to-day our lives have been marred by improprieties and sins. We have done those things which we ought not to have done, and we have left undone those things which we ought to have done, and there is no health in us. We do earnestly repent, and are heartily sorry for these our misdoings. The remembrance of them is grievous unto us. Have mercy upon us, most merciful Father. For thy Son our Lord Jesus Christ's sake, forgive us all that is past, and grant that we may ever hereafter serve and please thee in newness of life to the honor and glory of thy name, through Jesus Christ our Lord. And here we offer and present to thee, O Lord, ourselves, our souls and bodies, to be a reasonable, holy, and lively sacrifice unto thee, humbly beseeching thee that we all may be filled with thy grace and heavenly benediction. And although we be unworthy, through our manifold sins, to offer unto thee any sacrifice, yet we beseech thee to accept this our bounden duty and service, not weighing our merits, but pardoning our offenses through Jesus Christ our Lord, by whom and with whom, in the unity of the Holy Ghost, all honor and glory be unto thee, O Father Almighty, world without end. We implore thy blessings, most merciful Father, upon thy people everywhere. Give zeal and success to all who are laboring for the welfare of their fellows. Grant the Holy Spirit to those whom thou callest to the public ministry of the word. Encourage and help parents and teachers in the training and instruction of the young. Bless the editors of newspapers and the authors of books, that they may publish only such things as will benefit their readers. Give to our people at large proper views of life and duty, that they may desire that cultivation of their powers which will prepare them to fulfill their mission and be of service to their fellow-men. May temperance, sobriety, honesty, benevolence, and truth prevail in our land and in all lands, and may each one of us be instrumental in extending these principles among our friends and neighbors. Upon our absent relatives and friends, upon the dear ones who have asked an interest in our prayers, and upon all for whom we have promised to pray, command thy choicest blessings now to rest. May sweet sleep soon take possession of their weary limbs and ours, and after resting gently through the silent night, may we and they devote afresh to thee the remnant of our lives; and all the praise of our salvation shall be ever thine, O Father, Son, and Holy Ghost. Amen.

Go to the ant, thou sluggard; consider her ways, and be wise. These six things doth the Lord hate; yea, seven are an abomination unto him: A proud look, a lying tongue, and hands that shed innocent blood, a heart that deviseth wicked imaginations, feet that be swift in running to mischief, a false witness that speaketh lies, and him that soweth discord among brethren. Proverbs vi. 6, 16-19.

Services for Saturday Morning.

I. LESSON. 1 Thess. v. 1-18.

But of the times and the seasons, brethren, ye have no need that I write unto you. For yourselves know perfectly that the day of the Lord so cometh as a thief in the night. For when they shall say, Peace and safety; then sudden destruction cometh upon them, as travail upon a woman with child; and they shall not escape. But ye, brethren, are not in darkness, that that day should overtake you as a thief. Ye are all the children of light, and the children of the day; we are not of the night, nor of darkness. Therefore let us not sleep, as do others; but let us watch and be sober. For they that sleep sleep in the night; and they that be drunken are drunken in the night. But let us, who are of the day, be sober, putting on the breastplate of faith and love; and for a helmet, the hope of salvation. For God hath not appointed us to wrath, but to obtain salvation by our Lord Jesus Christ, who died for us, that, whether we wake or sleep, we should live together with him. Wherefore comfort yourselves together, and edify one another, even as also ye do. And we beseech you, brethren, to know them which labor among you, and are over you in the Lord, and admonish you; and to esteem them very highly in love for their work's sake. And be at peace among yourselves. Now we exhort you, brethren, warn them that are unruly, comfort the feeble-minded, support the weak, be patient toward all men. See that none render evil for evil unto any man; but ever follow that which is good, both among yourselves, and to all men. Rejoice evermore. Pray without ceasing. In every thing give thanks; for this is the will of God in Christ Jesus concerning you.

———

As for me, I will call upon God; and the Lord shall save me. Evening, and morning, and at noon, will I pray, and cry aloud; and he shall hear my voice. Cast thy burden upon the Lord, and he shall sustain thee; he shall never suffer the righteous to be moved.

Psalm lv. 16, 17, 22.

———

8,7,8,7,4,7.
GUIDE me, O thou great Jehovah,
  Pilgrim through this barren land;
I am weak, but thou art mighty;
  Hold me with thy powerful hand;
    Bread of heaven,
  Feed me till I want no more.

SATURDAY MORNING.

PRAYER.

ALMIGHTY GOD, our Heavenly Father, thy loving care has been over us through another night. We laid us down and slept, awoke and found thee near; and now with thankful hearts we praise thee, we give honor and glory unto thee; for great and marvelous are thy works, just and holy are thy ways. Thou hast remembered us through the darkness of the night, and hast brought us to behold the glad light of this morning, and to enjoy the privileges of another day. For thy preservation and watchful care over us we thank thee. May no worldly cares nor anxieties distract or disturb us in our morning worship, and may thy good providence go with us through this day and as long as life shall last. O Lord, we pray not for ourselves only, but for our absent ones, our kindred and friends, and for those who at any time have asked an interest in our prayers, and for all people. For Jesus' sake, show them thy mercy and loving-kindness; let thy light shine into their hearts, and may thy protection be over them. Preserve thy Church in truth and peace, against all enemies, through all trials; may she shine as the light of the world, and dispense her blessings to all mankind. Thy mercies are over all thy works. Be thou our keeper by day and by night. Preserve our souls and bodies from all evil; and may thy Spirit lead us into all truth and righteousness. These and all needed blessings we ask in the name of Jesus Christ our Lord. Amen.

II. LESSON. Eccles. xii. 1-7.

REMEMBER now thy Creator in the days of thy youth, while the evil days come not, nor the years draw nigh, when thou shalt say, I have no pleasure in them; while the sun, or the light, or the moon, or the stars, be not darkened, nor the clouds return after the rain; in the day when the keepers of the house shall tremble, and the strong men shall bow themselves, and the grinders cease because they are few, and those that look out of the windows be darkened, and the doors shall be shut in the streets, when the sound of the grinding is low, and he shall rise up at the voice of the bird, and all the daughters of music shall be brought low; also when they shall be afraid of that which is high, and fears shall be in the way, and the almond-tree shall flourish, and the grasshopper shall be a burden, and desire shall fail; because man goeth to his long home, and the mourners go about the streets; or ever the silver cord be loosed, or the golden bowl be broken, or the pitcher be broken at the fountain, or the wheel broken at the cistern. Then shall the dust return to the earth as it was; and the spirit shall return unto God who gave it.

C. M.

O MAY thy Spirit guide my feet
In ways of righteousness;
Make every path of duty straight
And plain before my face.

PRAYER.

ALMIGHTY GOD, our Heavenly Father, as we enter upon a new day we would humbly and devoutly renew our worship, our thanksgiving, our supplications, and our praises. We worship thee as the Infinite One, "glorious in holiness, fearful in praises, doing wonders;" we bless thee as the giver of all good gifts to thy creatures; we offer our supplications to thee as our prayer-hearing and prayer-answering God; we praise thee as the God of our salvation. As thy providence hath protected us from bodily harm during the darkness of the night, so may thy grace, O Lord, save us from all sin and all moral defilement during the day. May no evil come nigh unto us, and may all that touches our thought or our senses become a channel of grace to us through the power of thy indwelling Spirit. Help us to walk in the light as thou art in the light; make us strong in thy strength, that we may be able to carry the burdens laid on us; give us patience, that we may endure as seeing Him who is invisible; every moment enable us to exercise that faith which overcomes the world, and the charity that never faileth, and which will be our preparation and title to the inheritance of thy children in glory everlasting. Amen.

III. LESSON. Psalm cxlv. 8-19.

THE Lord is gracious, and full of compassion; slow to anger, and of great mercy. The Lord is good to all; and his tender mercies are over all his works. All thy works shall praise thee, O Lord; and thy saints shall bless thee. They shall speak of the glory of thy kingdom, and talk of thy power; to make known to the sons of men his mighty acts, and the glorious majesty of his kingdom. Thy kingdom is an everlasting kingdom, and thy dominion endureth throughout all generations. The Lord upholdeth all that fall, and raiseth up all those that be bowed down. The eyes of all wait upon thee; and thou givest them their meat in due season. Thou openest thine hand, and satisfiest the desire of every living thing. The Lord is righteous in all his ways, and holy in all his works. The Lord is nigh unto all them that call upon him, to all that call upon him in truth. He will fulfill the desire of them that fear him; he also will hear their cry, and will save them.

S. M.

Control my every thought;
My whole of sin remove;
Let all my works in thee be wrought,
Let all be wrought in love.

PRAYER.

O Lord, we thank thee for thy fatherly care over us during the past night; for the light of this new day; for the blessings of thy providence and grace. We feel our unworthiness and sinfulness in thy sight. Forgive our sins, we pray thee, and enable us to enter upon the duties of the day in thy fear and love. May the guiding hand of our God be upon us. May we have grace for the duties and trials of the day. May thy hand lead us, and thy arm defend us. Do thou bless the labor of our hands and the work we have to do. May the moments of the day be made up to us of innocence and love. O Lord, we pray that we may be cheerful, contented, and happy. May we have a Father's love, the communion of the Holy Spirit, and the peace of Christ abiding with us. May domestic duties and the business affairs of life be faithfully and pleasantly performed. May we so live and love, that when the day is past we shall have a satisfactory review, and feel that we are nearer the cross and heaven than we were at its beginning. We pray that the same blessings we have asked upon our house and home may rest upon all worshiping families, and all Christian people; that the riches of grace and the blessings of our Father may rest upon all states and conditions of men everywhere. We ask it all for Christ's sake. Amen.

IV. LESSON. 1 John iii. 1-8.

BEHOLD, what manner of love the Father hath bestowed upon us, that we should be called the sons of God; therefore the world knoweth us not, because it knew him not. Beloved, now are we the sons of God, and it doth not yet appear what we shall be; but we know that, when he shall appear, we shall be like him; for we shall see him as he is. And every man that hath this hope in him purifieth himself, even as he is pure. Whosoever committeth sin transgresseth also the law; for sin is the transgression of the law. And ye know that he was manifested to take away our sins; and in him is no sin. Whosoever abideth in him sinneth not; whosoever sinneth hath not seen him, neither known him. Little children, let no man deceive you; he that doeth righteousness is righteous, even as he is righteous. He that committeth sin is of the devil; for the devil sinneth from the beginning. For this purpose the Son of God was manifested, that he might destroy the works of the devil.

C. M.

Once more, my soul, the rising day
  Salutes thy waking eyes;
Once more, my voice, thy tribute pay
  To Him that rules the skies.

O God, let all my hours be thine,
  While I enjoy the light!
Then shall my sun in smiles decline,
  And bring a pleasant night.

PRAYER.

WE meet again, O Lord our God, to worship thee through Jesus Christ thy Son. Grant us thy Spirit, that we may worship thee aright. May our praises and our prayers come up acceptably before thee; and in response thereto may we enjoy fresh tokens of thy favor. Thy kind protection of us through another night gives us new cause for earnest gratitude to thee; and as thou raisest us to active life again, thou ceasest not to furnish us with all things needful for our bodies and our souls. For food and clothing, for air and water, for health and reason, for friends and kindred, for social intercourse and mutual love, we render hearty thanks to thee; but far above all these, and all thine other earthly gifts, we call upon our souls and all that is within us to bless thy holy name for hope of everlasting life on high. Help us to manifest our love to thee, not merely with our lips, but in our daily lives. Throughout this day especially may thy good Spirit follow us in all our paths. May he inspire us with constant gratitude for the constant blessings of thy providence which we receive. May he impart to us divine wisdom in the discharge of the difficult and delicate duties of life. May he restrain us from every thing unworthy of our calling and displeasing to thee. May he comfort us evermore with the assurance of our acceptance with thee through our Lord Jesus Christ. Enable us also to prove the reality of our love to thee by loving one another. Make us truly grateful to our dear friends who daily show us kindness. May we take pleasure in doing good to them as we have opportunity, serving them gladly in every proper way. Dispose us to contribute to their physical welfare, to their social enjoyment, to their mental improvement, but especially to their spiritual joy and salvation. And grant us grace, O Prince of Peace, to be so full of love supreme to thee that we may take delight in blessing even those who injure us. If our enemy hunger, may we feed him; if he thirst, may we give him drink, that in so doing we may heap coals of fire on his head. May we not be overcome of evil, but overcome evil with good. May the pure principles of the gospel of peace rapidly extend and soon prevail in all lands. May men be governed thereby in their personal dealings, in public affairs, and in all international concerns. May it soon come to pass that thy Son shall judge among the nations and shall rebuke many people; and they shall beat their swords into plowshares and their spears into pruning-hooks, and nation shall not lift up sword against nation, neither shall they learn war any more. Bless all proper efforts to extend the kingdom of thy Son. Give earnestness and zeal to all thy servants, clerical and lay. May all the members of thy Church submit themselves and all they have to thy control. Help those women who are laboring in the gospel to send its elevating, saving influences to their sisters still degraded and enslaved in heathen lands. Impress the hearts of the children that they may early begin to work in thy vineyard, so that they may grow in grace and in the knowledge of our Lord and Saviour Jesus Christ. Bless the President of the United States, and all others in authority. May all kings reign in righteousness and princes rule in judgment, that the people may lead quiet and peaceable lives in all godliness and honesty; and may all classes of men rejoice in the fact that thou reignest supreme. And now, O Lord, attend unto our cry, give ear unto our prayer that goeth not forth out of feigned lips; for all we offer is in Jesus' name. Amen.

ASK, and it shall be given you; seek, and ye shall find; knock, and it shall be opened unto you; for every one that asketh recciveth; and he that seeketh findeth; and to him that knocketh it shall be opened. Matthew vii. 7, 8.

Services for Saturday Evening.

I. LESSON. Psalm xxiii.

The Lord is my shepherd; I shall not want. He maketh me to lie down in green pastures; he leadeth me beside the still waters. He restoreth my soul; he leadeth me in the paths of righteousness for his name's sake. Yea, though I walk through the valley of the shadow of death, I will fear no evil; for thou art with me; thy rod and thy staff they comfort me. Thou preparest a table before me in the presence of mine enemies; thou anointest my head with oil; my cup runneth over. Surely goodness and mercy shall follow me all the days of my life; and I will dwell in the house of the Lord forever.

L. M.

Now all chafing care shall cease,
Now worn toil obtain release,
With the world we now have done,
Since "the Sabbath draweth on."

PRAYER.

Our Father in heaven, we thank thee for the blessings of the week now closing. Thou hast given us life and health, and food and clothing, and many other blessings. Thou hast brought us through the perils of the week, and we are still preserved by thy kind and effectual care. Now that the day of rest is near, deliver us from all that has vexed and excited us, and give us thy peace, that we may be prepared to worship with reverence and devout fear. We pray thee to forgive the sins of the week. Enter not into judgment with us, that our thoughts and feelings and words and acts have not been holy and pleasing to thee. We come before thee in the name of Jesus, and would appropriate to ourselves his perfect righteousness, and pray that for his sake our consciences may be cleansed and our hearts renewed in righteousness. Bless with us all who are dear to us— our relatives, friends, and neighbors. Bless the Church to which we belong, and those who minister to us in holy things. Unite all who name the name of Christ in one hope and faith and love, and extend thy kingdom until every knee shall bow to thee and every tongue confess thy name. Defend us from the dangers of the night, and give us refreshing sleep, for thou, O Father, only makest us to dwell in safety. These and all other blessings we ask in the name of Jesus Christ our Lord and Saviour. Amen.

II. LESSON. Matthew v. 1-12.

AND seeing the multitudes, he went up into a mountain; and when he was set, his disciples came unto him; and he opened his mouth, and taught them, saying, Blessed are the poor in spirit; for theirs is the kingdom of heaven. Blessed are they that mourn; for they shall be comforted. Blessed are the meek; for they shall inherit the earth. Blessed are they which do hunger and thirst after righteousness; for they shall be filled. Blessed are the merciful; for they shall obtain mercy. Blessed are the pure in heart; for they shall see God. Blessed are the peace-makers; for they shall be called the children of God. Blessed are they which are persecuted for righteousness' sake; for theirs is the kingdom of heaven. Blessed are ye, when men shall revile you, and persecute you, and shall say all manner of evil against you falsely, for my sake. Rejoice, and be exceeding glad; for great is your reward in heaven; for so persecuted they the prophets which were before you.

C. M.

TALK with us, Lord, thyself reveal,
  While here o'er earth we rove;
Speak to our hearts, and let us feel
  The kindling of thy love.

PRAYER.

Almighty God, for Christ's sake, have mercy on us and save our souls. We are poor, weak creatures, and need grace and mercy every day. Jesus, remember us, and wash us in thy precious blood. God be merciful to us sinners. O our God, we pray thee to be kept from sin, the world and the devil. We cannot keep ourselves, for we have no power or might of our own. Put thy Holy Spirit in our hearts, and let us not fall. Hold thou us up, and we shall be safe. Strengthen us for all our duties. Give us grace to do all that we have to do faithfully, honestly, and well, as to the Lord and not to man. May we be truthful, sober, diligent, kind, good-tempered, and wise, in every place and in every company. Bless our country with peace and good government. Bless the Church to which we belong, and the congregation of which we are members. Pour out the Holy Spirit on the community in which we live, and increase true religion here and everywhere. Above all, bless all our family, relations, and friends. May all have what is good for them in this life and the grace of God in their hearts. And may we all meet at last in a heavenly home, to part no more. Amen.

III. LESSON. Malachi iii. 1-12.

BEHOLD, I will send my messenger, and he shall prepare the way before me; and the Lord, whom ye seek, shall suddenly come to his temple, even the messenger of the covenant, whom ye delight in; behold, he shall come, saith the Lord of hosts. But who may abide the day of his coming? and who shall stand when he appeareth? for he is like a refiner's fire, and like fullers' soap; and he shall sit as a refiner and purifier of silver; and he shall purify the sons of Levi, and purge them as gold and silver, that they may offer unto the Lord an offering in righteousness. Then shall the offering of Judah and Jerusalem be pleasant unto the Lord, as in the days of old, and as in former years. And I will come near to you to judgment; and I will be a swift witness against the sorcerers, and against the adulterers, and against false swearers, and against those that oppress the hireling in his wages, the widow, and the fatherless, and that turn aside the stranger from his right, and fear not me, saith the Lord of hosts. For I am the Lord, I change not; therefore ye sons of Jacob are not consumed. Even from the days of your fathers ye are gone away from mine ordinances, and have not kept them. Return unto me, and

I will return unto you, saith the Lord of hosts. But ye said, Wherein shall we return? Will a man rob God? Yet ye have robbed me. But ye say, Wherein have we robbed thee? In tithes and offerings. Ye are cursed with a curse; for ye have robbed me, even this whole nation. Bring ye all the tithes into the storehouse, that there may be meat in mine house, and prove me now herewith, saith the Lord of hosts, if I will not open you the windows of heaven, and pour you out a blessing, that there shall not be room enough to receive it. And I will rebuke the devourer for your sakes, and he shall not destroy the fruits of your ground; neither shall your vine cast her fruit before the time in the field, saith the Lord of hosts. And all nations shall call you blessed; for ye shall be a delightsome land, saith the Lord of hosts.

C. M.

I LOVE to steal awhile away
   From every cumb'ring care;
And spend the hours of setting day
   In humble, grateful prayer.

I love to think on mercies past,
   And future good implore;
And all my cares and sorrows cast
   On Him whom I adore.

PRAYER.

WE thank thee, our Heavenly Father, for all thy goodness to us. Our lives are the gift of thy love, and all the temporal and spiritual blessings that we have ever enjoyed have come from thee. Increase in us the spirit of gratitude, and save us from the curse of thankless hearts. We acknowledge our sins, and we trust that we are sincerely sorry for them. Without excuse of any sort, and in the face of light and knowledge, we have gone astray from thee. We have sinned in thought and word and deed. Our hearts condemn us, and thou art greater than our hearts. O help us to repent, and then, for Jesus' sake, pardon and forgive. Send thy Holy Spirit into our hearts to bear witness with our spirits that we are thy children. Let the fruit of the Spirit abound in us. Cleanse us from all defilement, and give us constant fellowship with thee. Grant us the perfect love that casts out all fear. Then shall our lights shine brightly before our fellow-men. Sanctify our home life. Bless us also in our association with our fellow-men, and help us to be diligent, wise, upright, and kind in every place and in every company. Bless our absent loved ones. Give them such things as are best for them in this life, and especially bestow upon them all spiritual blessings in heavenly places in Christ Jesus. We would not forget those who have asked us to pray for them. Thou knowest their needs; supply them all according to the riches of thy grace in Christ Jesus. Accept these our prayers, and at last in heaven save us for his sake. Amen.

IV. LESSON. Romans v. 1-10.

THEREFORE being justified by faith, we have peace with God through our Lord Jesus Christ; by whom also we have access by faith into this grace wherein we stand, and rejoice in hope of the glory of God. And not only so, but we glory in tribulations also; knowing that tribulation worketh patience; and patience, experience; and experience, hope; and hope maketh not ashamed; because the love of God is shed abroad in our hearts by the Holy Ghost which is given unto us. For when we were yet without strength, in due time Christ died for the ungodly. For scarcely for a righteous man will one die; yet peradventure for a good man some would even dare to die. But God commendeth his love toward us, in that, while we were yet sinners, Christ died for us. Much more then, being now justified by his blood, we shall be saved from wrath through him. For if, when we were enemies, we were reconciled to God by the death of his Son; much more, being reconciled, we shall be saved by his life.

C. M.

How sad our state by nature is!
Our sin how deep it stains!
And Satan binds our captive souls
Fast in his slavish chains.

But there's a voice of sovereign grace
Sounds from the sacred word;
Ho! ye despairing sinners, come,
And trust a faithful Lord.

PRAYER.

O Lord, our Father and our God, thou hast kindly lengthened out our lives, unworthy and unfaithful though they have been; and now, on the eve of the Sabbath, after ceasing from the active labors of the week, we come together unto thee for fresh supplies of grace and mercy from on high. Thou art the source of all our pure and perfect joy, and from our infancy thou hast supplied our varied wants from thine unwasting fullness. During the week now closing we have had from day to day fresh proofs that thou art willing still to bless all those who put their trust in thee. We earnestly desire to offer thee to-night a sacrifice of gratitude and praise through Jesus Christ our Lord, which we humbly pray thee to receive, and give us a consciousness of our connection with thee and evidence of our acceptance in thy sight. May we be in perfect sympathy with thy gracious plans concerning us and our fellow-men; may we cheerfully comply with the reasonable terms on which thou offerest to men pardon and peace and everlasting life; and may we deem it our highest joy to be employed in some capacity in furthering the interests of thy cause and kingdom. Grant grace and unction from above to all who may be called to preach thy word to-morrow. Indue them plenteously with heavenly gifts. May cloven tongues like as of fire rest on their hearts, that those who hear their earnest words may understand the heavenly language and comprehend the lesson of thy love. May many on this coming Sabbath-day renounce their idols and their sins, and set their faces Zionward. Embrace within thy loving arms to-night, O Father, all the human race. Thou knowest perfectly the needs of every living thing. Be merciful to all—the high, the low, the rich, the poor, the bond, the free, the pious, the profane, those who accept and those who spurn the offer of salvation. To all who suffer bodily affliction give thy sustaining grace. Be thou the father of the fatherless and the judge of the widows. Soften the hearts of rich men, that they may give of their abundance to relieve the worthy poor. Heavenly Father, regard with tender interest the rising race. May parents feel the vast importance of their relation to their offspring. Grant to all mothers strength of character, that they may wield their mighty influence for the present welfare and everlasting happiness of their precious charge. May those who undertake to train their neighbors' children in colleges and schools discharge their arduous duties in thy fear, so that by thy help and blessing the children may escape all hurtful influences and be prepared for useful stations in the Church and State. Again we pray thy blessings on our absent friends and kindred. May thine all-seeing eye follow them for good, and may they all be faithful unto death, that thou mayest give to each of them a crown of life. And now, glory be to the Father, and to the Son, and to the Holy Ghost, as it was in the beginning, is now, and ever shall be, world without end. Amen.

PRAYER FOR OPENING SUNDAY-SCHOOL.

O Lord, our Father, we have come from our homes, to hear what thou wilt say to us to-day. Open our hearts and minds, that we may gladly learn thy will as taught us in our present lesson. May we not desire merely to know the meaning of the words we read, but may we rather treasure in our hearts the precious truths contained therein, and learn to enjoy that higher wisdom which comes down from heaven. May we put far from us every evil thing; and may these children devote themselves to thee in early life. Help us this day, this very hour, with earnest sorrow for our sins, to trust the precious merits of our Saviour Jesus Christ, and feel that for his sake our sins are pardoned and our souls are blessed. And now, O Father, bless us as a school. Be with us in our songs of praise and in our Scripture lessons, and in our humble prayers. And in all we do, may it be our constant object to promote the glory of thy holy name. And unto thee, O Father, Son, and Holy Ghost, be praise and glory forever and ever. Amen.

PRAYER FOR CLOSING SUNDAY-SCHOOL.

O Lord, our Heavenly Father, we humbly pray thee to impress upon our minds and hearts the lessons we have learned to-day, that we may practice them in all our future lives. May we all grow wiser and better as we grow older, and become better prepared and better disposed for the duties of life as long as thou shalt spare us on the earth. Be with us all and bless us through the coming week, and bring us to our school again next Sunday, prepared for further lessons from thy holy word. Guide us in all our ways through future life; and when our work on earth is done, receive us to thyself on high, for Jesus' sake. Amen.

PRAYER FOR OPENING WOMAN'S MISSIONARY MEETING.

O LORD, our Heavenly Father, we adore thee for the gift of Jesus Christ, thy Son our Lord, to be the Saviour of mankind. We bless thee that thou didst so love the world that thou didst give thine only-begotten Son that whosoever believeth in him should not perish, but have everlasting life. We praise thee for the high position given to our sex in all those lands to which the glad tidings of the gospel have thus far come. We thank thee that thou hast cast our lot in an enlightened land, where we enjoy the common blessings of our Christian civilization, and the hopes of everlasting life, revealed to us through Jesus Christ our Lord. We lament the degradation of our benighted sisters, who still bow in blind idolatry to stocks and stones, worshiping they know not what, and enslaved by a debasing and cruel superstition. We recognize their claim to our sympathy and help, and we have come together to-day to implore divine direction and encouragement in our humble efforts to elevate and save the heathen women of the world. We thank thee, O merciful Father, for the general interest now pervading the Christian Church on the duty of sending the gospel to the heathen. We bless thee for the efforts and contributions made by the Church at large, and especially for those of the women and the children made for the special benefit of the women and the children who are still without the gospel. Wilt thou encourage and stimulate this spirit, that it may intensify and spread till we who feel it now may far more deeply feel our obligation to deny ourselves and devote ourselves to the spread of thy kingdom in the earth, and till all who are in reach of the blessings of the gospel may be induced to help, as far as in them lies, in imparting to others the blessings they enjoy. Bestow thy richest blessings, we beseech thee, O Lord, upon our dear sisters who have left their native land, and are laboring in distant regions to propagate the truth as it is in Jesus Christ. Encourage them in their work of faith and labor of love. Give them the satisfaction of seeing thy work prospering in their hands. Through their instrumentality, accompanied by the gracious influences of the Holy Ghost, may many men and women renounce their idols and devote themselves to thee. And raise up native helpers, who shall go abroad among their countrymen, and recommend to all the heavenly hopes they have been taught to entertain. Thus may the time be near at hand when all the earth shall know thee, and rejoice in hope of thy coming glory. And now, O Father, be present with us while we remain together. May we all feel that it is good to be here. May we enjoy a comfortable assurance of our acceptance with thee, and a well-founded hope of those heavenly joys to which we invite our benighted fellows. And may the exercises of this occasion tend to the glory of thy name, and the extension of thy cause among the children of men. And to thy great and glorious name, O Father, Son, and Holy Ghost, be praise and glory, now and forever. Amen.

Praise God, from whom all blessings flow;
Praise him, all creatures here below;
Praise him above, ye heavenly host;
Praise Father, Son, and Holy Ghost.

CHILD'S PRAYER.

Jesus, take this heart of mine;
Make it pure and wholly thine;
Thou hast bled and died for me,
I will henceforth live for thee.

CHILD'S MORNING PRAYERS.

The morning bright with rosy light
  Has waked me from my sleep;
Father, I own thy love alone
  Thy little one doth keep.
All through the day, I humbly pray,
  Be thou my guard and guide;
My sins forgive, and let me live,
  Blest Jesus, near thy side.
All this I ask for Jesus' sake.   Amen.

Now I awake and see the light.
'Tis God has kept me through the night;
To him I lift my voice and pray
That he would keep me through the day;
And when on earth my work is done,
O God, accept me through thy Son.

CHILD'S EVENING PRAYERS.

Now I lay me down to sleep,
I pray the Lord my soul to keep;
If I should die before I wake
I pray the Lord my soul to take.
All this I ask for Jesus' sake. Amen.

SAVIOUR, tender Shepherd, hear me;
 Bless thy little lamb to-night;
Through the darkness be thou near me,
 Watch my sleep till morning light.

All this day thy hand hath led me,
 And I thank thee for thy care;
Thou hast clothed me, warmed me, fed me—
 Listen to my evening prayer.

Let my sins be all forgiven,
 Bless the friends I love so well;
Take me, when I die, to heaven,
 Happy there with thee to dwell.
All this I ask for Jesus' sake. Amen.

THE LORD'S PRAYER.

OUR Father, who art in heaven, hallowed be thy name: thy kingdom come: thy will be done on earth as it is in heaven: give us this day our daily bread; and forgive us our trespasses, as we forgive those who trespass against us; and lead us not into temptation, but deliver us from evil; for thine is the kingdom, and the power, and the glory, forever and ever. Amen.

BIBLE PRAYERS.

The Holy Scriptures contain many beautiful expressions of prayer which will be found suggestive as models both of the spirit and form of worship. We insert a few, with the hope that they will be frequently read, and will inspire feelings of devotion and reverence; and that this little book, instead of superseding the Bible in the family, may awaken more interest in it as a volume of inspired truth—"all of which is profitable for doctrine, for reproof, for correction, for instruction in righteousness."

Give ear to my words, O Lord; consider my meditation. Hearken unto the voice of my cry, my King, and my God; for unto thee will I pray. (Ps. v. 1, 2.)

Let the words of my mouth and the meditation of my heart, be acceptable in thy sight, O Lord, my strength, and my redeemer. (Ps. xix. 14.)

Thy mercy, O Lord, is in the heavens; and thy faithfulness reacheth to the clouds. Thy righteousness is like the great mountains; thy judgments are a great deep; O Lord, thou preservest man and beast. How excellent is thy loving-kindness, O God! therefore the children of men put their trust under the shadow of thy wings. They shall be abundantly satisfied with the fatness of thy house; and thou shalt make them drink of the river of thy pleasures. For with thee is the fountain of life; in thy light shall we see light. O continue thy loving-kindness unto them that know thee, and thy righteousness to the upright in heart. (Ps. xxxvi. 5-10.)

Lord, thou hast been our dwelling-place in all generations. Before the mountains were brought forth, or ever thou hadst formed the earth and the world, even from everlasting to everlasting, thou art God. (Ps. xc. 1, 2.)

Blessed be the God and Father of our Lord Jesus Christ, who hath blessed us with all spiritual blessings in heavenly places in Christ. (Eph. i. 3.)

Thy throne, O God, is forever and ever; a scepter of righteousness is the scepter of thy kingdom. Thou hast loved righteousness, and hated iniquity; therefore God, even thy God, hath anointed thee with the oil of gladness above thy fellows. (Heb. i. 8, 9.)

Great and marvelous are thy works, Lord God Almighty; just and true are thy ways, thou King of saints. Who shall not fear thee,

O Lord, and glorify thy name? for thou only art holy; for all nations shall come and worship before thee; for thy judgments are made manifest. (Rev. xv. 3, 4.)

I acknowledge my transgressions; and my sin is ever before me. Behold, I was shapen in iniquity; and in sin did my mother conceive me. Behold, thou desirest truth in the inward parts; and in the hidden part thou shalt make me to know wisdom. Purge me with hyssop, and I shall be clean; wash me, and I shall be whiter than snow. Hide thy face from my sins, and blot out all mine iniquities. Create in me a clean heart, O God; and renew a right spirit within me. Cast me not away from thy presence; and take not thy Holy Spirit from me. Restore unto me the joy of thy salvation; and uphold me with thy free Spirit. (Ps. li. 3, 5–7, 9–12.)

O Lord, righteousness belongeth unto thee, but unto us confusion of faces, because we have sinned against thee. To the Lord our God belong mercies and forgivenesses, though we have rebelled against him; neither have we obeyed the voice of the Lord our God, to walk in his laws. (Daniel ix. 7, 8–10.)

Father, I have sinned against heaven, and

in thy sight, and am no more worthy to be called thy son. (Luke xv. 21.)

Show me thy ways, O Lord; teach me thy paths. Lead me in thy truth, and teach me; for thou art the God of my salvation; on thee do I wait all the day. Remember, O Lord, thy tender mercies and thy loving-kindnesses; for they have been ever of old. Remember not the sins of my youth, nor my transgressions; according to thy mercy remember thou me, for thy goodness' sake, O Lord. (Ps. xxv. 4–7.)

Lord, be merciful unto me; heal my soul; for I have sinned against thee. (Ps. xli. 4–7.)

Give us help from trouble; for vain is the help of man. (Ps. lx. 11.)

So teach us to number our days, that we may apply our hearts unto wisdom. O satisfy us early with thy mercy; that we may rejoice and be glad all our days. (Ps. xc. 12, 14.)

Lord, save us; we perish. (Matt. viii. 25.)

Lord, help me. (Matt. xv. 25.)

Lord, I believe; help thou mine unbelief. (Mark ix. 24.)

God be merciful to me a sinner. (Luke xviii. 13.)

God be merciful unto us, and bless us, and cause his face to shine upon us; that thy way may be known upon earth, thy saving health among all nations. Let the people praise thee, O God; let all the people praise thee. O let the nations be glad and sing for joy; for thou shalt judge the people righteously, and govern the nations on earth. Let the people praise thee, O God; let all the people praise thee. Then shall the earth yield her increase; and God, even our own God, shall bless us. God shall bless us; and all the ends of the earth shall fear him. (Ps. lxvii.)

Into thine hand I commit my spirit; thou hast redeemed me, O Lord God of truth. (Ps. xxxi. 5.)

Whom have I in heaven but thee? and there is none upon earth that I desire besides thee. My flesh and my heart faileth; but God is the strength of my heart, and my portion forever. (Ps. lxxiii. 25, 26.)

O Lord, truly I am thy servant; I am thy servant, and the son of thy handmaid; thou hast loosed my bonds. I will offer to thee the sacrifice of thanksgiving, and will call upon the name of the Lord. I will pay my vows unto the Lord now in the presence of all his people, in the courts of the Lord's house, in the midst of thee, O Jerusalem. Praise ye the Lord. (Ps. cxvi. 16–19.)

I am thine, save me. (Ps. cxix. 94.)

Blessed be thou, Lord God of Israel our father, forever and ever. Thine, O Lord, is the greatness, and the power, and the glory, and the victory, and the majesty; for all that is in the heaven and in the earth is thine; thine is the kingdom, O Lord, and thou art exalted as head above all. Both riches and honor come of thee, and thou reignest over all; and in thine hand is power and might; and in thine hand it is to make great, and to give strength unto all. Now, therefore, our God, we thank thee, and praise thy glorious name. (1 Chron. xxix. 10–13.)

O Lord, I will praise thee; though thou wast angry with me, thine anger is turned away, and thou comfortedst me. (Isa. xii. 1.)

Glory to God in the highest, and on earth peace, good-will toward men. (Luke ii. 14.)

O the depth of the riches both of the wisdom and knowledge of God! how unsearchable are his judgments, and his ways past finding out! For who hath known the mind of the Lord? or who hath been his counselor? Or who hath first given to him, and it shall be recompensed unto him again? For of him, and to him, are all things; to whom be glory forever. Amen. (Rom. xi. 33–36.)

Now unto him that is able to do exceeding abundantly above all that we ask or think, according to the power that worketh in us, unto him be glory in the Church by Christ Jesus throughout all ages, world without end. Amen. (Eph. iii. 20, 21.)

Now unto the King eternal, immortal, invisible, the only wise God, be honor and glory forever and ever. Amen. (1 Tim. i. 17.)

Unto him that loved us, and washed us from our sins in his own blood, and hath made us kings and priests unto God and his Father; to him be glory and dominion forever and ever. Amen. (Rev. i. 5, 6.)

Blessing, and honor, and glory, and power, be unto him that sitteth upon the throne, and unto the Lamb forever and ever. (Rev. v. 13.)

BENEDICTIONS.

THE Lord bless thee, and keep thee; the Lord make his face shine upon thee, and be gracious unto thee; the Lord lift up his countenance upon thee, and give thee peace. (Num. vi. 24–26.)

Now the God of hope fill you with all joy and peace in believing, that ye may abound in hope, through the power of the Holy Ghost. (Rom. xv. 13.)

The grace of the Lord Jesus Christ, and the love of God, and the communion of the Holy Ghost, be with you all. Amen. (2 Cor. xiii. 14.)

Grace be with all them that love our Lord Jesus Christ in sincerity. Amen. (Eph. vi. 24.)

Now unto God and our Father be glory forever and ever. Amen. (Phil. iv. 20.)

Grace be unto you, and peace, from God our Father and the Lord Jesus Christ. (Col. i. 2.)

Now our Lord Jesus Christ himself, and God, even our Father, which hath loved us, and hath given us everlasting consolation and good hope through grace, comfort your hearts, and stablish you in every good word and work. (2 Thess. ii. 16, 17.)

Now the Lord of peace himself give you peace always by all means. The Lord be with you all. (2 Thess. iii. 16.)

Grace be with you all. Amen. (Titus iii. 15.)

Now the God of peace, that brought again from the dead our Lord Jesus, that great Shepherd of the sheep, through the blood of the everlasting covenant, make you perfect in every good work to do his will, working in you that which is well-pleasing in his sight, through Jesus Christ; to whom be glory forever and ever. Amen. (Heb. xiii. 20, 21.)

But the God of all grace, who hath called us unto his eternal glory by Christ Jesus, after that ye have suffered awhile, make you perfect, stablish, strengthen, settle you. To him be glory and dominion forever and ever. Amen. (1 Peter v. 10, 11.)

Now unto him that is able to keep you from falling, and to present you faultless before the presence of his glory with exceeding joy, to the only wise God our Saviour, be glory and majesty, dominion and power, both now and ever. Amen. (Jude 24, 25.)

Grace be unto you, and peace, from him which is, and which was, and which is to come; and from the seven Spirits which are before his throne; and from Jesus Christ, who is the faithful witness, and the first-begotten of the dead, and the prince of the kings of the earth. (Rev. i. 4, 5.)

The grace of our Lord Jesus Christ be with you all. Amen. (Rev. xxii. 21.)

GRACES BEFORE MEAT

Heavenly Father, pardon our sins, and grant us grateful hearts for these and all thy blessings, we ask for Christ's sake. Amen.

We bless thee, our gracious Father, for these refreshments; and may thy blessing and thy peace abide upon this house and in all our hearts, we humbly beg for Christ's sake. Amen.

Sanctify our food and conversation, O Lord, forgive all our sins, and save us at last in heaven, for Christ's sake. Amen.

GRACES AFTER MEAT.

Accept our grateful acknowledgments, Heavenly Father, for these and all thy blessings, we humbly ask for Christ's sake. Amen.

Our Father in heaven, we have again been fed by thy bounty. Wilt thou continue thy blessings and feed us with the bread of life. While we live may we live to thy glory, and finally be admitted into thy kingdom, for Christ's sake. Amen.

The Ten Commandments:
With Parallel Texts.

FIRST COMMANDMENT.

AND God spake all these words, saying, I am the Lord thy God, which have brought thee out of the land of Egypt, out of the house of bondage. Thou shalt have no other gods before me. Exodus xx. 1-3.

These words the Lord spake unto all your assembly in the mount out of the midst of the fire, of the cloud, and of the thick darkness, with a great voice; and he added no more. And he wrote them in two tables of stone, and delivered them unto me. (Deut. v. 22.) I am the Lord thy God from the land of Egypt, and thou shalt know no god but me; for there is no savior besides me. (Hos. xiii. 4.) Go not after other gods to serve them, and ye shall dwell in the land which I have given to you and to your fathers. (Jer. xxxv. 15.) Go not after other gods to serve them, and to worship them, and provoke me not to anger with the works of your hands. (Jer. xxv. 6.) Ye shall not go after other gods, of the gods of the people which are round about you. (Deut. vi. 14.) With Israel the Lord had made a covenant, and charged them, saying, Ye shall not fear other gods, nor bow yourselves to them, nor serve them, nor sacrifice to them. (2 Kings xvii. 35.) Of a truth, Lord, the kings of Assyria have destroyed the nations and their lands, and have cast their gods into the fire; for they were no gods, but the work of men's hands, wood and stone; therefore they have destroyed them. (2 Kings xix. 17, 18.) Though there be that are called gods, whether in heaven or in earth (as there be gods many, and lords many), but to us there is but one God, the Father, of whom are all things, and we in him. (1 Cor. viii. 5, 6.)

SECOND COMMANDMENT.

Thou shalt not make unto thee any graven image, or any likeness of any thing that is in heaven above, or that is in the earth beneath, or that is in the water under the earth: thou shalt not bow down thyself to them, nor serve them; for I the Lord thy God am a jealous God, visiting the iniquity of the fathers upon the children unto the third and fourth generation of them that hate me; and shewing mercy unto thousands of them that love me, and keep my commandments. Exodus xx. 4-6.

Lest ye corrupt yourselves, and make you a graven image, the similitude of any figure, the likeness of male or female. (Deut. iv. 16.) Cursed be the man that maketh any graven or molten image, an abomination unto the Lord, the work of the hands of the craftsman, and putteth it in a secret place. And all the people shall answer and say, Amen. (Deut. xxvii. 15.) Confounded be all they that serve graven images, that boast themselves of idols; worship him, all ye gods. (Ps. xcvii. 7.) Ye shall drive out all the inhabitants of the land from before you, and destroy all their pictures, and destroy all their molten images, and quite pluck down all their high places. (Num. xxxiii. 52.) Thou shalt not bow down to their gods, nor serve them. (Ex. xxiii. 24.) Neither make mention of the name of their gods, nor cause to swear by them, neither serve them, nor bow yourselves unto them. (Josh. xxiii. 7.)

Thou shalt worship no other god; for the Lord, whose name is Jealous, is a jealous God. (Ex. xxxiv. 14.) The Lord thy God is a consuming fire, even a jealous God. (Deut. iv. 24.) I will not give my glory unto another. (Isa. xlviii. 11.) Joshua said unto the people, Ye cannot serve the Lord; for he is a holy God;

he is a jealous God; he will not forgive your transgressions nor your sins. (Josh. xxiv. 19.) Wherefore I will yet plead with you, saith the Lord, and with your children's children will I plead. (Jer. ii. 9.) By no means clearing the guilty, visiting the iniquity of the fathers upon the children unto the third and fourth generation. And your children shall wander in the wilderness forty years, and bear your whoredoms, until your carcasses be wasted in the wilderness. (Num. xiv. 18, 33.) God layeth up his iniquity for his children. (Job xxi. 19.) I will set my face against that man, and against his family. (Lev. xx. 5.) And they that are left of you shall pine away in their iniquity in your enemies' lands; and also in the iniquities of their fathers shall they pine away with them. If they shall confess their iniquity, and the iniquity of their fathers, with their trespass which they trespassed against me, and that also they have walked contrary unto me; and that I also have walked contrary unto them, and have brought them into the land of their enemies; if then their uncircumcised hearts be humbled, and they then accept of the punishment of their iniquity; then will I remember my covenant with Jacob, and also my covenant with Isaac, and also my covenant with Abraham will I remember; and I will remember the land: (Lev. xxvi. 39–42.) Seest thou how Ahab humbleth himself before me? because he humbleth himself before me, I will not bring the evil in his days; but in his son's days will I bring the evil upon his house. (1 Kings xxi. 29.) The seed of the evil-doers shall never be renowned. Prepare slaughter for his children for the iniquity of their fathers. (Isa. xiv. 20, 21.) ·Behold, it is written before me: I will not keep silence, but will recompense, even recompense into their bosom, your iniquities, and the iniquities of your fathers together, saith the Lord. (Isa. lxv. 6, 7.)

O remember not against us former iniquities. (Ps. lxxix. 8.) Know therefore that the Lord thy God, he is God, the faithful God, which keepeth covenant and mercy with them that love him and keep his commandments to a thousand generations. (Deut. vii. 9.) My covenant will I not break, nor alter the thing that is gone out of my lips. (Ps. lxxxix. 34.) He that hath my commandments, and keepeth them, he it is that loveth me; and he that loveth me shall be loved of my Father, and I will love him, and will manifest myself to him. (John xiv. 21.) As touching the election, they are beloved for the fathers' sakes. (Rom. xi. 28.)

Who is a God like unto thee, that pardoneth iniquity, and passeth by the transgression of the remnant of his heritage? he retaineth not his anger forever, because he delighteth in mercy. He will turn again, he will have compassion upon us; he will subdue our iniquities; and thou wilt cast all their sins into the depths of the sea. Thou wilt perform the truth to Jacob, and the mercy to Abraham, which thou hast sworn unto our fathers from the days of old. (Micah vii. 18–20.) Thou shewest loving-kindness unto thousands, and recompensest the iniquity of the fathers into the bosom of their children after them; The Great, The Mighty God, The Lord of hosts, is his name. (Jer. xxxii. 18.) O Lord, the great and dreadful God, keeping the covenant and mercy to them that love him, and to them that keep his commandments. (Dan. ix. 4.)

THIRD COMMANDMENT.

Thou shalt not take the name of the Lord thy God in vain; for the Lord will not hold him guiltless that taketh his name in vain.

Exodus xx. 7.

Lord, who shall abide in thy tabernacle? who shall dwell in thy holy hill? He that walketh uprightly, and worketh righteousness, and speaketh the truth in his heart. He that backbiteth not with his tongue, nor doeth evil to his neighbor, nor taketh up a reproach against his neighbor. In whose eyes a vile person is contemned; but he honoreth them that fear the Lord. He that sweareth to his own hurt, and changeth not. He that putteth not out his money to usury, nor taketh reward against the innocent. He that doeth these things shall never be moved. (Ps. xv. 1–5.) Put not thine hand with the wicked to be an unrighteous witness. (Ex. xxiii. 1.) Ye shall not swear by my name falsely, neither shalt thou profane the name of thy God; I am the Lord. (Lev. xix. 12.) He that blasphemeth the name of the Lord, he shall surely be put to death. (Lev. xxiv. 16.) Ye have heard that it hath been said by them of old time, Thou shalt not forswear thyself, but shalt perform unto the Lord thine oaths; but I say unto you, Swear not at all; neither by heaven, for it is God's throne; nor by the earth, for it is his footstool; neither by Jerusalem, for it is the city of the great King. Neither shalt thou swear by thy head, because thou canst not make one hair white or black. But let your communication be, Yea, yea; Nay, nay; for whatsoever is more than these cometh of evil.

(Matt. v. 33–37.) But above all things, my brethren, swear not, neither by heaven, neither by the earth, neither by any other oath; but let your yea be yea; and your nay, nay; lest ye fall into condemnation. (James v. 12.)

FOURTH COMMANDMENT.

REMEMBER the Sabbath-day, to keep it holy. Six days shalt thou labor, and do all thy work; but the seventh day is the Sabbath of the Lord thy God; in it thou shalt not do any work, thou, nor thy son, nor thy daughter, thy man-servant, nor thy maid-servant, nor thy cattle, nor thy stranger that is within thy gates: for in six days the Lord made heaven and earth, the sea, and all that in them is, and rested the seventh day; wherefore the Lord blessed the Sabbath-day, and hallowed it.　　Exodus xx. 8-11.

Six days thou shalt do thy work, and on the seventh day thou shalt rest; that thine ox and thine ass may rest, and the son of thy handmaid, and the stranger, may be refreshed. (Ex. xxiii. 12.) Six days may work be done; but in the seventh is the Sabbath of rest, holy to the Lord; whosoever doeth any work in the Sabbath-day, he shall surely be put to death. (Ex. xxxi. 15.) Six days shall work be done;

but the seventh day is the Sabbath of rest, a holy convocation; ye shall do no work therein; it is the Sabbath of the Lord in all your dwellings. (Lev. xxiii. 3.) Six days thou shalt work, but on the seventh day thou shalt rest; in earing time and in harvest thou shalt rest. (Ex. xxxiv. 21.) Six days ye shall gather manna; but on the seventh day, which is the Sabbath, in it there shall be none. (Ex. xvi. 26.) The ruler of the synagogue answered with indignation, because that Jesus had healed on the Sabbath-day, and said unto the people, There are six days in which men ought to work; in them therefore come and be healed, and not on the Sabbath-day. (Luke xiii. 14.) In the sweat of thy face shalt thou eat bread, till thou return unto the ground. (Gen. iii. 19.)

Not slothful in business; fervent in spirit; serving the Lord. (Rom. xii. 11.) Let him that stole steal no more; but rather let him labor, working with his hands the thing which is good, that he may have to give to him that needeth. (Eph. iv. 28.) Neither did we eat any man's bread for naught; but wrought with labor and travail night and day, that we might not be chargeable to any of you; not because we have not power, but to make ourselves an ensample unto you to follow us. For even when we were with you, this we commanded you, that if any would not work, neither should he eat. (2 Thess. iii. 8–10.) On the seventh day God ended his work which he had made; and he rested on the seventh day from all his work which he had made. And God blessed the seventh day, and sanctified it; because that in it he had rested from all his work which God created and made. (Gen. ii. 2, 3.) I gave them my Sabbaths, to be a sign between me and them, that they might know that I am the Lord that sanctify them. (Ezek. xx. 12.) Verily my Sabbaths ye shall keep. (Ex. xxxi. 13.) In the first day ye shall have a holy convocation; ye shall do no servile work therein. (Lev. xxiii. 7.) There dwelt men of Tyre also therein, which brought fish, and all manner of ware, and sold on the Sabbath unto the children of Judah, and in Jerusalem. Then I contended with the nobles of Judah, and said unto them, What evil thing is this that ye do, and profane the Sabbath-day? And it came to pass, that when the gates of Jerusalem began to be dark before the Sabbath, I commanded that the gates should be shut, and charged that they should not be opened till after the Sabbath; and some of my servants set I at the gates, that there should no burden be brought in on the Sabbath-day. (Neh. xiii. 16, 17, 19.) Keep my Sabbaths; I am the Lord your God. Ye shall keep my Sabbaths, and reverence my sanctuary; I am the Lord. (Lev. xix. 3, 30.)

FIFTH COMMANDMENT.

Honor thy father and thy mother; that thy days may be long upon the land which the Lord thy God giveth thee. Exodus xx. 12.

Honor thy father and thy mother, as the Lord thy God hath commanded thee; that thy days may be prolonged, and that it may go well with thee, in the land which the Lord thy God giveth thee. (Deut. v. 16.) God commanded, saying, Honor thy father and mother, and he that curseth father or mother, let him die the death. (Matt. xv. 4; Mark vii. 10.) Honor thy father and mother; which is the first commandment with promise. (Eph. vi. 2.) Whoso curseth his father or his mother, his lamp shall be put out in obscure darkness. (Prov. xx. 20.) Ye shall fear every man his mother, and his father, and keep my Sabbaths. I am the Lord your God. (Lev. xix. 3.) And Jeremiah said unto the house of the Rechabites, Thus saith the Lord of hosts, the God of Israel: Because ye have obeyed the commandment of Jonadab your father, and kept all his precepts, and done according unto all that he hath commanded you; therefore thus saith the Lord of hosts, the God of Israel: Jonadab the son of Rechab, shall not want a man to stand before me forever. (Jer. xxxv. 18, 19.)

SIXTH COMMANDMENT.

Thou shalt not kill.   Exodus xx. 13.

Whoso sheddeth man's blood, by man shall his blood be shed; for in the image of God made he man. (Gen. ix. 6.) The devil was a murderer from the beginning. (John viii. 44.) Out of the heart proceed evil thoughts, murders, adulteries, fornications, thefts, false witness, blasphemies. (Matt. xv. 19.) Cain talked with Abel his brother; and it came to pass, when they were in the field, that Cain rose up against Abel his brother, and slew him. And the Lord said unto Cain, Where is Abel thy brother? And he said, I know not; am I my brother's keeper? And he said, What hast thou done? the voice of thy brother's blood crieth unto me from the ground. And now art thou cursed from the earth, which hath opened her mouth to receive thy brother's blood from thy hand. When thou tillest the ground, it shall not henceforth yield unto thee her strength; a fugitive and a vagabond shalt thou be in the earth. (Gen. iv. 8–12.) Thou hast killed Uriah the Hittite with the sword, and hast taken his wife to be thy wife, and hast slain him with the sword of the children of Ammon. (2 Sam. xii. 9.) Deliver me from blood-guiltiness, O God, thou God of my salvation; and my tongue shall sing aloud of thy righteousness. (Ps. li. 14.) Ye have heard that it was said by them of old time, Thou shalt not kill; and whosoever shall kill shall be in danger of the judgment; but I say unto you, That whosoever is angry with his brother without a cause shall be in danger of the judgment; and whosoever shall say to his brother, Raca, shall be in danger of the council; but whosoever shall say, Thou fool, shall be in danger of hell-fire. (Matt. v. 21, 22.) Let none of you suffer as a murderer, or as a thief. (1 Pet. iv. 15.)

SEVENTH COMMANDMENT.

THOU shalt not commit adultery.

Exodus xx. 14.

The sword shall never depart from thine house; because thou hast despised me, and hast taken the wife of Uriah the Hittite to be thy wife. (2 Sam. xii. 10.) But I say unto you, That whosoever looketh on a woman to lust after her hath committed adultery with her already in his heart. (Matt. v. 28.) The mouth of strange women is a deep pit; he that is abhorred of the Lord shall fall therein. (Prov. xxii. 14.) Give not thy strength unto women, nor thy ways to that which destroyeth kings. (Prov. xxxi. 3.) When I had fed them to the full, they then committed adultery, and assembled themselves by troops in the harlots' houses. They were as fed horses in the morning; every one neighed after his neighbor's wife. Shall I not visit for these things? saith the Lord; and shall not my soul be avenged on such a nation as this? (Jer. v. 7–9.) Whoredom and wine and new wine take away the heart. (Hos. iv. 11.) Whosoever shall put away his wife, except it be for fornication, and shall marry another, committeth adultery. (Matt. xix. 9.) The works of the flesh are manifest, which are these: Adultery, fornication, uncleanness, lasciviousness, idolatry, witchcraft, hatred, variance, emulations, wrath, strife, seditions, heresies, envyings, murders, drunkenness, revelings, and such like; of the which I tell you before, as I have also told you in time past, that they which do such things shall not inherit the kingdom of God. (Gal. v. 19–21.)

Let no corrupt communication proceed out of your mouth, but that which is good to the use of edifying, that it may minister grace unto the hearers. (Eph. iv. 29.) Fornication, and all uncleanness, or covetousness, let it not be once named among you, as becometh saints; neither filthiness, nor foolish talking, nor jesting, which are not convenient; but rather giving of thanks. For this ye know, that no whoremonger, nor unclean person, nor covetous man, who is an idolater, hath any inheritance in the kingdom of Christ and of God. Let no man deceive you with vain words; for because of these things cometh the wrath of God upon the children of disobedience. Be not ye therefore partakers with them. (Eph. v. 3-7.) Mortify therefore your members which are upon the earth; fornication, uncleanness, inordinate affection, evil concupiscence. (Col. iii. 5.) Not in the lust of concupiscence, even as the Gentiles which know not God; for God hath not called us unto uncleanness, but unto holiness. (1 Thess. iv. 5, 7.) Marriage is honorable in all, and the bed undefiled, but whoremongers and adulterers God will judge. (Heb. xiii. 4.) The Lord knoweth how to deliver the godly out of temptations, and to reserve the unjust unto the day of judgment to be punished; but chiefly them that walk after the flesh in the lust of uncleanness, and despise government. But these, as natural brute beasts, made to be taken and destroyed, speak evil of the things that they understand not; and shall utterly perish in their own corruption. Having eyes full of adultery, and that cannot cease from sin. (2 Pet. ii. 9, 10, 12, 14.) Even as Sodom and Gomorrah, and the cities about them in like manner, giving themselves over to fornication, and going after strange flesh, are set forth for an example, suffering the vengeance of eternal fire. But these speak evil of those things which they know not; but what they know naturally, as brute beasts, in those things they corrupt themselves. (Jude 7, 10.)

EIGHTH COMMANDMENT.

THOU shalt not steal.   Exodus xx. 15.

Ye shall not steal, neither deal falsely, neither lie one to another. Thou shalt not defraud thy neighbor, neither rob him; the wages of him that is hired shall not abide with thee all night until the morning. (Lev. xix. 11, 13.) Neither shalt thou steal. (Deut. v. 19.) If a man shall steal an ox, or a sheep, and kill it, or sell it, he shall restore five oxen for an ox, and four sheep for a sheep. If a thief be found breaking up, and be smitten that he die, there shall no blood be shed for him. If the sun be risen upon him, there shall be blood shed for him; for he should make full restitution; if he have nothing, then he shall be sold for his theft. If the theft be certainly found in his hand alive, whether it be ox, or ass, or sheep; he shall restore double. (Ex. xxii. 1-4.) Rob not the poor, because he is poor; neither oppress the afflicted in the gate; for the Lord will plead their cause, and spoil the soul of those that spoiled them. (Prov. xxii. 22, 23.) He that by usury and unjust gain increaseth his substance, he shall gather it for him that will pity the poor. Whoso robbeth his father or his mother, and saith, It is no transgression; the same is the companion of a destroyer. (Prov. xxviii. 8, 24.) Nor thieves, nor covetous, nor drunkards, nor revilers, nor extortioners, shall inherit the kingdom of God. (1 Cor. vi. 10.) Let no man go beyond and defraud his brother in any matter; because that the Lord is the avenger of all such, as we also have forewarned you and testified. (1 Thess. iv. 6.) Let him that stole steal no more; but rather let him labor, working with his hands the thing which is good, that he may have to give to him that needeth. (Eph. iv. 28.)

NINTH COMMANDMENT.

Thou shalt not bear false witness against thy neighbor. Exodus xx. 16.

Put not thine hand with the wicked to be an unrighteous witness. (Ex. xxiii. 1.) Neither shalt thou bear false witness against thy neighbor. (Deut. v. 20.) If a false witness rise up against any man to testify against him that which is wrong; then shall ye do unto him, as he had thought to have done unto his brother; so shalt thou put the evil away from among you. (Deut. xix. 16, 19.) Lord, who shall abide in thy tabernacle? Who shall dwell in thy holy hill? He that walketh uprightly, and worketh righteousness, and speaketh the truth in his heart. He that backbiteth not with his tongue, nor doeth evil to his neighbor, nor taketh up a reproach against his neighbor. In whose eyes a vile person is contemned; but he honoreth them that fear the Lord. He that sweareth to his own hurt, and changeth not. (Ps. xv. 1–4.) Whoso privily slandereth his neighbor, him will I cut off. (Ps. ci. 5.) Deliver me not over unto the will of mine enemies; for false witnesses are risen up against me, and such as breathe out cruelty. (Ps. xxvii. 12.) Thou shalt not raise a false report; put not thine hand with the wicked to be an unrighteous witness. (Ex. xxiii. 1.) And I will come near to you to judgment; and I will be a swift witness against the sorcerers, and against the adulterers, and against false swearers, and against those that oppress the hireling in his wages, the widow and the fatherless, and that turn aside the stranger from his right, and fear not me, saith the Lord of hosts. (Mal. iii. 5.)

TENTH COMMANDMENT.

Thou shalt not covet thy neighbor's house, thou shalt not covet thy neighbor's wife, nor his man-servant, nor his maid-servant, nor his ox, nor his ass, nor any thing that is thy neighbor's. Exodus xx. 17.

Neither shalt thou desire thy neighbor's wife, neither shalt thou covet thy neighbor's house, his field, or his man-servant, or his maid-servant, his ox, or his ass, or any thing that is thy neighbor's. (Deut. v. 21.) Whosoever looketh on a woman to lust after her, hath committed adultery with her already in his heart. (Matt. v. 28.) Can a man take fire in his bosom, and his clothes not be burned? Can one go upon hot coals, and his feet not be burned? so he that goeth in to his neighbor's wife; whosoever toucheth her shall not be innocent. (Prov. vi. 27-29.) Woe to him that coveteth an evil covetousness to his house, that he may set his nest on high, that he may be delivered from the power of evil. (Hab. ii. 9.) I had not known sin, but by the law; for I had not known lust, except the law had said, Thou shalt not covet. (Rom. vii. 7.) Let your conversation be without covetousness; and be content with such things as ye have; for he hath said, I will never leave thee, nor forsake thee. (Heb. xiii. 5.) Take heed and beware of covetousness; for a man's life consisteth not in the abundance of the things which he possesseth. (Luke xii. 15.) I have coveted no man's silver, or gold, or apparel. (Acts xx. 33.) Fornication, and all uncleanness, or covetousness, let it not be once named among you, as becometh saints. For this ye know, that no whoremonger, nor unclean person, nor covetous man, who is an idolater, hath any inheritance in the kingdom of Christ and of God. (Eph. v. 3, 5.)

—

My son, keep my words, and lay up my commandments with thee. Keep my commandments, and live; and my law as the apple of thine eye. Bind them upon thy fingers, write them upon the table of thine heart. Say unto wisdom, Thou art my sister; and call understanding thy kinswoman. Proverbs vii. 1-4.

SCRIPTURAL READINGS—COVETOUSNESS.

My kingdom is not of this world. (John xviii. 36.)

And he said unto them, Take heed, and beware of covetousness; for a man's life consisteth not in the abundance of the things which he possesseth. (Luke xii. 15.)

He also that received seed among the thorns is he that heareth the word; and the care of this world, and the deceitfulness of riches, choke the word, and he becometh unfruitful. (Matt. xiii. 22.) The love of money is the root of all evil; which while some coveted after, they have erred from the faith, and pierced themselves through with many sorrows. (1 Tim. vi. 10.) A little that a righteous man hath is better than the riches of many wicked. (Ps. xxxvii. 16.) Godliness with contentment is great gain. For we brought nothing into this world, and it is certain we can carry nothing out. And having food and raiment, let us be therewith content. (1 Tim. vi. 6–8.) Better is little with the fear of the Lord, than great treasure and trouble therewith. (Prov. xv. 16.)

Lay not up for yourselves treasures upon earth, where moth and rust doth corrupt, and where thieves break through and steal; but lay up for yourselves treasures in heaven, where neither moth nor rust doth corrupt, and where thieves do not break through nor steal; for where your treasure is, there will your heart be also. (Matt. vi. 19-21.)

And he spake a parable unto them, saying, The ground of a certain rich man brought forth plentifully; and he thought within himself, saying, What shall I do, because I have no room where to bestow my fruits? And he said, This will I do: I will pull down my barns, and build greater; and there will I bestow all my fruits and my goods. And I will say to my soul, Soul, thou hast much goods laid up for many years; take thine ease, eat, drink, and be merry. (Luke xii. 16-19.)

But God said unto him, Thou fool, this night thy soul shall be required of thee; then whose shall those things be which thou hast provided? (Luke xii. 20.)

So is he that layeth up treasure for himself, and is not rich toward God. (Luke xii. 21.)

Charge them that are rich in this world, that they be not high-minded, nor trust in uncertain riches, but in the living God, who giveth us richly all things to enjoy; that they do good, that they be rich in good works, ready to distribute, willing to communicate; laying up in store for themselves a good foundation against the time to come, that they may lay hold on eternal life. (1 Tim. vi. 17–19.) Hath not God chosen the poor of this world rich in faith, and heirs of the kingdom which he hath promised to them that love him? (James ii. 5.) Be careful for nothing; but in every thing by prayer and supplication with thanksgiving let your request be made known unto God. (Phil. iv. 6.)

Therefore take no thought, saying, What shall we eat? or, What shall we drink? or, Wherewithal shall we be clothed? (for after all these things do the Gentiles seek); for your heavenly Father knoweth that ye have need of all these things. But seek ye first the kingdom of God, and his righteousness; and all these things shall be added unto you. Take therefore no thought for the morrow; for the morrow shall take thought for the things of itself. Sufficient unto the day is the evil thereof. (Matt. vi. 31–34.)

I have been young, and now am old; yet have I not seen the righteous forsaken, nor his seed begging bread. (Ps. xxxvii. 25.)

The kingdom of God is not meat and drink; but righteousness, and peace, and joy in the Holy Ghost. (Rom. xiv. 17.)

READINGS FOR SPECIAL OCCASIONS.

The following readings are suggested for special occasions:

Advent: The Messiah in Prophesy—Isaiah lxi. 1-11.

Christ the Comforter in Prophesy—Isaiah xl. 1-11.

Christ the Comforter in the Gospel—John xiv. 15, 16.

Good Friday.—Isaiah liii. 13.

Christ's Resurrection: Easter Sunday—1 Corinthians xv. 1-58.

Thanksgiving—Psalms viii., xviii., xxxiii., lxv., lxvii., lxxxiv., lxxxv., xcv., xcvi., xcvii., civ., cvii., cxviii., cxxxvi.

Time of Trouble—Psalms xxviii., lxxxvi.; Lamentations iii.

Hope and Trust—Psalms xxvii., xl.

Confidence—Psalms xxxvii., xlvi., lxii., lxxi.

Missionary Occasions—Isaiah liv., lx.

Counsels and Suggestions—Proverbs vi. 1-22; xv. 1-20; Romans xii.; Ephesians iv. 17-32; v. 1-21; vi. 1-20; Colossians iii. 1-25.

Temptations of the Tongue—James iii.

Getting Wisdom—Proverbs iv. 5-27.

Hope of Glory—2 Corinthians v. 15.

Charity—1 Corinthians xiii. 1-21.

www.ingramcontent.com/pod-product-compliance
Lightning Source LLC
Chambersburg PA
CBHW021841230426
43669CB00008B/1035